WRITING WITH THE *INFINITE SPIRIT*
By
Carol S. Batey, Ph.D.

Dedication

This book is dedicated to all aspiring authors who want to learn how to enhance their writing under the influence of Non-physical beings and *Infinite Spirit*. Use your inner powers to tap into the Source of all things under heaven and Earth. This is your God-given right to exercise this wonderful power that helps you to create as it comes through you!

This is a guidebook on how to develop intimacy and encourages a communion with the *Infinite Spirit* for writing your books. We all are creative expressions of the universal God who has equipped us with unseen beings to assist our writing task, if we ask. We all are illuminated light energy and guidance is given unto our soul and mind by the inner still, small voice once we tap into it. Seek the assistance in a reverence for your writing journey through silence, meditation, affirmative prayer and thanksgiving in humility. This book was called forth for you, dear reader. Warm wishes to you all.

Notes about the Author

As a minister, I was delighted to look through the content exposition and see the direction Dr. Batey was taking with the intention behind this book. It is, itself, a perfect example of inspired writing, and it spoke from her heart and to mine. There is so much to be said for allowing Spirit to express itself in, and through, us. Inspiration in alignment with the Divine flow shares a Truth that only our particularized point of expression may shine.

This book beautifully walks you through the process of connecting with that sacred muse, allowing it to become your very essence, and unleashing your power of imagination and creativity. I am impressed with the care and consideration given to being informative and comprehensive, while still being personal and authentic. There is great power in "letting go" and translating the very deepest, and often lightest, experiences into words. Each of us has a truth that is universal, and that's what makes writing so powerful. In some way, everyone can connect with the core of being that one may lovingly bring to the table with their writing.

I was touched by the final chapter about the author's disillusionment with her mother, and the bridge to another inner guide that proved to be a new channel from which the *Infinite Spirit* expressed. This rings true with a genuine feel that can only be accomplished by using the very tools discussed in the chapter, "Be True to What You Believe." Getting to our inner Truth and letting go of any intellectual notions of what we should or shouldn't express is what captivates the reader. What do YOU have to say? I know that the very worst times of my own life were the very best springboards for the discovery of my own beliefs. This makes me who I am, and propels me forward in my own writing. The Spirit is

in everything, and this book shows us how to allow the Spirit to guide us on our way to writing down in words the glory of God as Us.
- Reverend Scott De Marco, New Thought Spiritual Center, Cincinnati, OH

    Rev. Dr. Carol S. Batey and her 2011 book, "Why Aren't You Writing," came into my life as an answer to a fervent prayer. This new project that she is, I believe, channeling, is full of valuable spiritual guidance and inspiration for aspiring writers who have a spiritual calling or mission. "Writing with the *Infinite Spirit*" is truly going to bless and encourage a new wave of writers who yearn to share the Divine messages that are coming through them to a world waiting to be blessed by them.
- Evelyn B. Bourne, Spiritual Blogger and Author of *31 Intentions*

Table of Contents

Dedication	2
Notes about the Author	4
Author's Welcome - Sunday, September 5	8
Introduction	13
Chapter 1 - Writing with the *Infinite Spirit*	25
Chapter 2 - Let It Be	38
Chapter 3 - Staying in the Writing Zone	52
Chapter 4 - Welcome Success with te Help of the *Infinite Spirit*	75
Chapter 5 - Personal Soul Journal	100
Chapter 6 - Desire, Expect, Believe	107
Chapter 7 - Finding My Way to Spiritual Freedom	118
Chapter 8 - Research is a Must	133
Chapter 9 - Marketing and Promotions with an Omnipresent Source	148
Chapter 10 - Be True To What You Believe	163
Chapter 11 - All Things are Spiritual: Destiny's Calling Your Soul	171
Chapter 12 - Questions and Answers: The Discovery	179
Chapter 13 - Saint Teresa, One of My Writing Partners	187
Afterthought	200
About the Author	204
Acknowledgements	209

"The best writer has no lace on his sleeves."
- Walt Whitman (1819-1892)

Author's Welcome

Sunday, September 5

My dearest writer, it is my fondest dream that you receive the message within this book. Please keep an open heart and mind on how you may start or enhance your writing projects with the guidance of the Infinite Spirit. I totally believe in this subject matter. If not, it wouldn't be presented in this book. The messages given within this book are very personal and private to me. I feel ever so vulnerable unveiling my innermost secrets! Cherish them.

I attend First Church Unity in Nashville, Tennessee, which is a part of the Unity movement. My belief system is one of New Thought Christian, which was created around the 19th century in the United States. Unity was co-created by Charles and Myrtle Fillmore with a strong focus in the Bible and mind-healing. I have always believed in the Holy Trinity--Father, Son and the Holy Spirit and still do. Just recently, I completed my doctoral degree at the University of Metaphysics in April 2011. My doctoral studies were in Mystical Research.

I share the Christian religion with many others, yes, but I have an enlarged my view of Spiritual Realities, perhaps in comparison with most believers. I have an understanding of Truth that embraces uncommon ideas or, at least ideas that are not much discussed in the Christian traditions. Ever since I was a child, I saw and felt the presence of angels and other non-physical beings. When I was a child, there was no one to help me understand what I was seeing or to share this information with. As long as I can remember, I knew things beyond my age and wisdom and was able to see death upon others. Not only did I see death, I could sense happiness as well. For example, my ex- husband and I have six children; he only wanted two children. I saw all six children on a picture when there were only two of them present. Also, I have always had premonitions and hunches of things going on in the lives of others and my own life. At one point in time, years ago, my son Joshua ran away from home around age 12. I asked my Dad, Fred who was deceased, where Joshua went. I got the strong impression where to look for him and he was found safely. I am blessed to have the Infinite Spirit living within my soul which speaks to me in a still, small voice! Within this book, I share my private stories of the invisible spirits that assist and provide tools to aid my writing task. They are angels, power Spirit animals and, of course, the *Infinite Spirit*. The invisible spirits are also non-physical guides and teachers that help equip us humans with special knowledge and unconditional love.

    Dearest Writer, anyone who may feel they are called to write a book may not be called to become a channel to get a message out to the public. Every book is just not going to sell to the public on a large scale. Some writers are called to write to leave a family legacy while many are called to write at least one hour daily in their personal soul journal, Smartphone or personal computer. Whatever the case may be, just make sure you keep a daily personal soul journal, express your soulful thoughts and, thus, provide inner healing for yourself. I can attest that when I wished I had someone to talk with about issues I was having I wrote. There was not anyone for me to communication my deepest thoughts, too. Whether you are writing to be published or not, you are writing under the influence of the Infinite Spirit, angels, and non-physical beings, if you are mindful and welcome the assistance. Unlock your words within your mind and Spirit to paper. That's good therapy and is needed for all.

For those of you who know you are called to publish, write and market your project to the world, move forward. Working with the non-physical guides, you will be able to understand processes that you did not previously know. For instance, if you do not know how a train works, you will be able to understand this knowledge with the help of a non-physical guide. For me, I think of it as someone unseen is guiding my hands when I am writing or typing on my personal computer. Then, I sense there is another feeling, as if someone is pouring information into my mind, just like when a computer downloads information. This pouring happens to my mind when I know I really didn't know the information before hand. One non-physical teacher which I know to be one of my teachers is Saint Teresa of Avila. She helps me to understand my spiritual life purposes. This teacher helped me understand that my life-purpose is to write books to others no matter what I thought my limitations were. She also is a non-physical teacher who brings me to the inner knowing of my own soul. Many times I, like her, thought I was a stupid person and that I didn't have the smarts to write anything. Then, when I would have doubts and fears, I read her words and I would find inner knowledge and wisdom. I found comfort and a solace in her admitting her own shortcomings and limitations.

    One of main ideas of communing with the Infinite Spirit, angels or non-physical beings is the practice of emptying one's self to a power Higher than their self; as well as putting a daily spiritual practice or personal soul journal in place, so that the channels of good will flow to you and through you. You will read in almost every account of the chapters on the importance of implementing a spiritual practice of silence, meditation, prayer and personal soul journal. I do know that we all have non-physical angels, guides and teachers to assist us on this Earthly journey. We are never alone; we just think and feel that we are alone. These light energy beings agreed together that they would provide guidance and protection for us until we leave this Earthly plane. We must then ask for their assistance, so please do. They source us with so much knowledge, wisdom, direction, guidance, protection and, most of all, unconditional love. The non-physical beings love us humans no matter what we do, say or think. They are pure love and energy. The gift of unconditional love to friends, family members and those you don't know is given to another person no matter what a person does in their life. A person may not believe in other's personal beliefs or actions, but they are loved by others anyway. This is unconditional love because unconditional love does not push, control or make another person think, act or feel any other way to get love. Most of all, there is the unconditional love of *Infinite Spirit* to humanity no matter what humans have done. Unconditional love is always present no matter what has occurred.

    This book is my design about my own experience on this Earth at this time working and writing with the Infinite Spirit. This book has been called forth out of necessity for those who are ready to receive it with the essential message of conversing and attunement with the *Infinite Spirit* while creating their writing projects! If you are reading this timely message it is because it was written just for your soul. Enjoy the soul journey and let me know how this book has impacted your life. For those of you that find your writing has been a struggle, then tap into the Divine inspiration of the unseen beings for ease and grace. In the name of my Blessed Lord Jesus, Amen.

Introduction

Writing with the Infinite Spirit

"O do you think that I cannot pray to My Father and He will provide me with more than twelve legions of angels."
- Matt: 26:53; KJV

As you start this writing journey in how to develop an intimacy and communion with the Infinite Spirit, you will gain blessings beyond measure. Just know you will be given more than twelve legions of angels to guide you as you write, but understand the invitation must be extended to them. The word Infinite means; never ending, unlimited, unbound, endless and boundless; now do you get the picture? Whatever your faith/belief; most people believe in a Spirit or God higher than or greater themselves. Other words used to describe Spirit are *Infinite Spirit*, Deity, God, Divinity, Supernatural Spirit, Universal Mind or Intelligence. This book is a direct creation from teaching many writing workshops where students asked the central question, "How do I learn to write with, and under the influence of, God or Spirit?"

Someone else asked me a similar question on this subject, "Carol, have you ever been tapped while sleeping by unseen beings to get up right then to write?" A student started their task of writing, and asked, "Where are the words coming from and what if I don't get enough to fill a page?"

Then, there are those who have an uncertainty of what is occurring within their psyche soul. They start examining. The writer hears messages, promptings within their soul, and sees inner visions of scenes and doesn't understand the mystery. The Spirit's language is unknown to their souls; they try to analyze. Students come to me as a teacher and they ask important questions of their soul. The Zen proverb states, "When the student is ready; the teacher will appear." I can't assume that you understand what Zen means. It's from a form of Buddhism, which its main focus on meditation and enlightenment.

In humility, I can only give them insights of my own personal experience of writing with the Infinite Spirit. I research many media for internal answers for myself and for others. It is my passion and I love getting up in the middle of the night to research and read to gain clarity. In the meantime, I have learned to attune myself in the silence, and through meditation, prayer, discipline and profound love for my Higher Power to hear answers. When that happens for me, I am able to hear from the legions of helpers that are unseen to me. Clearly, I feel them closely and welcome their input in my writing projects.

On other occasions, I have read other authors' experiences about their spiritual encounters on the same subject. Joel S. Goldsmith, author of *The Heart of Mysticism: The Infinite Way Letters* (2007), has shared with his readers that he recalled being asleep and then awakened by the Holy Spirit to get out of bed to write. When he finished and returned to bed, he awoke again later only to find he wrote messages that he would learn from. I know he's not the only author who has written under the influence of the Holy Spirit. You too, may experience the same; do not be surprised. If you desire a similar experience ask *Infinite Spirit* before you retire to bed for this dream state to happen to you.

My dear writer, don't think that you have to enter into a monastery in order to learn the language of reverence of your inner soul. Reverence is a form of high honor. It comes into your heart as you create and put into action "spiritual practice" daily. This "spiritual practice" is done in simplicity with an inner reverence toward your God. There is really no place for you to go to enter into a prayer presence. Accept your own soul. You don't have to become a monk, nun, hermit, or minister unless it is your desire to answer that call. You can be a devotee of the Infinite Spirit without leaving your career, home, or family life. Another word of advice; you don't have to leave your spiritual faith or rich traditions to learn how to commune with the *Infinite Spirit* for your book project or writings. The purpose of this book is for you to enhance the rich process of writing under the influence of the *Infinite Spirit*. This means writing with something beyond us that will create a product that's so magnificent!

    Each one of us in this world is to be a unique expression of the Universal God. There are many people who aren't aware that this concept is true. How we express this unique gift is different from one to another. We have free will to choose our good and perfect gifts. Again, within this text, we are focusing on the process of writing under the influence of the Infinite Spirit. One must understand we are spiritual beings always, living a human experience. We are not alone in this world even though it may appear this is so. Little children have seen angels and most adults haven't always believed their children; and therefore, start to suppress their visions. Then, on the other hand, there are sensitive adults whose inner senses are so keen that they have seen angels often. Throughout the ages of time, the prophets, sages, mystics, philosophers, saints, and just ordinary people have been directed and protected by hosts of angels, many of whom they have been very aware. Angels are the messengers and workers of the *Infinite Spirit* who assist us writers and humans.

Each and every one of us on this planet has Infinite Spirits; not just the Holy Spirit, but angels along with many non-physical teachers and guides, this includes non-physical animal spirits, too. As we become clear channels (body, mind and Spirit), and spiritual vessels, they work through us in direct communication. Transfer knowledge of inspiration from the ancient masters and sages is given to us by a feeling, word, dream, nudging, sound, smell, color, a still small voice within, or a prompting. Artists, ministers, writers, physicians, parents and musicians and more have relied on this channel of pure inspiration with zeal and fervor for creating anything. Thomas Carlyle (1795-1881) stated: "Music is well said to be the speech of angels." I believe angelic speech can be anything the muse inspires and can encompass everything in our lives. It is up to us to "trust the process" and the inspiration our hearts. Then, we need to trust our minds and the Universal Mind. Universal Mind is the same name for "God" or "*Infinite Spirit.*" The meaning is the same--all knowing, most powerful, all creative, and ever present. One person in my class from a traditional faith asked me, "How does the Universal Mind work?" My comment was simply that Universal Mind works just like God or *Infinite Spirit*, even though the term may be different from what you are familiar with. Nonetheless, these non-physical guides and teachers give us guidance, comfort, love, protection and wish the best for our success. They live in the Spirit realm. We are not alone, though in a love of solitude and silence and an inward focus on the spiritual life, a writer can be peaceful and find security. These non-physical guides and teachers may be from a past lifetime.

Nevertheless, our non-physical guides are brilliant and talented friends, masters, and most of all, our mentors on this Earth. Non-physical guides and teachers may assist us for a short period of time or a lifetime. With each writing project, one may get new guides or teachers to assist them along their writing path, and it is my personal belief that familiar ones may be kept. When these non-physical guides and teachers on the other side decide that something is needed on this Earthly realm, a human person brings the informative message through. The significant messages are transmuted to our souls and then our minds.

Gary Zukav, author of *The Seat of the Soul* (1990), shares how non-physical teachers bring us closer to knowing our soul and how non-physical guides help us with major projects. If you are one who is to write about aircrafts, then you may call into your reality a guide for assistance. Saint Teresa of Avila, a Spanish nun from the sixteen century, is a non-physical teacher and guide who has helped people understand the yearnings of their inner soul. I am one that she helps daily. I sense and feel her company speaking to me. Through her mystical literary works, she gives a spiritual blueprint to others on how to develop a mystic consciousness and how to stay connected to the beloved. It does not matter if you don't know your guides' or teachers' names. Just know that they are there for you helping with your writing project.

Teachers and guides that are non-physical energy have lived life in human form and may know us since they have lived in one or more lifetimes. They also understand our human life and can relate to us easily; therefore, they are ready to assist. "For He shall give his angels charge over thee, to keep thee in all thy ways" (Psalms 91:11; KJV). We all know, as we have read from the Holy Bible, how important angels are to God. Angels carry out the will and messages of the Infinite Spirit. Again, they give guidance to humans in visions, with words and messages to write, and they give meanings to dreams, give praise, and worship their Deity. Angels, in contrast, have never had a physical body; they have never been human. Numerous people have heard about some of the Archangels like Michael, Uriel, Raphael or Gabriel; I know there are a few more. This is not a book on angels; we will focus only on the four. However, if you would like to understand more, I suggest reading *The Angel Book* (1993) by Karen Goldman.

    Dear Writer, you have the illuminated light within your soul and you have been guided always by the still small voice. Maybe you have been unaware of the light workers who assist us beyond the veil. To me, 'beyond the veil' means having knowledge of another world beyond our physical Earthly plane; a life beyond this one. Most people think the term 'beyond the veil' refers to an afterlife or life beyond death, which is true. Some religions and cultures believe that humans come to Earth with a veil over their eyes that they can't see the Spirit world all around us.

    Therefore, become a seeker and look for communication in your daily life, world and affairs. Cling to the inner passions of your soul, by not being so preoccupied by the Earthly cares of this world. It is a challenge, believe me. I have to refocus daily on living a spiritual life. Don't allow your human passions and desires to control you. Seek a reverence for spiritual things by making a progress through silence and meditation with no thought of time, or concerns of where you are. Once you come out of that inward practice, revelations from your inner kingdom can be given unto you. Give an affirmative thanks for your secret prayers of your heart and mind that answers have been given for your writings.

The Infinite Spirit's secrets are revealed to the humble and draw the person's mind and heart ever so close. Then, be reluctant to speak of your findings aloud to another. Conversely, let these findings simmer in your soul for a while. Afterwards, you will know within that the message was from the *Infinite Spirit* without any doubts. In that moment, start to write your feelings or the messages out on paper. Trust your inner guidance and as you focus on this process; more will be given unto you. You have begun to become a spiritual writer whether it is non-fiction or fiction! All inspired writings are channeled through the *Infinite Spirit* to a willing vessel.

The Source of all things is the Infinite Spirit. In everything, give thanks. Jim Pym's book, *Listening to the Light* (2000), tells of the author's personal experience of becoming a Quaker. He is still a committed Roman Catholic and practices Buddhism, but he is also a Friend in Quakerism. He is not the only one to admit being so attracted to the Quaker faith. George Fox, the founder of Quakerism, read and knew the Qur'an and quoted it when speaking with Muslims. The attraction for those who practice Quakerism is that their meetings are a silent worship. Members of this faith sit in silence on Sunday just to be in the presence of God. This practice for them is not just a Sunday routine; it can happen anywhere they are in a "sacred space." The inner experience for the Quakers is a waiting on God. We, too, may get inspiration from their example and from Fox.

How often do you commune with another person: a loved one, nature, animals--specifically all of *Infinite*

Spirit's creations? This action of entering into the silence is no different except you are communing with the Divine *Infinite Spirit*. When I write, I speak to my audience of diverse religious groups and spirituality, all races, both genders, ages (21 and up) and various demographics. It is my prayer that those who have an open mind will hear the message written in my words. My written message is non-threatening because I set my intentions for that order while writing by holding a sacred space for that action. As a spiritual writer, it is my intent to raise a level of spiritual consciousness of how the *Infinite Spirit* works in our lives, regardless of what the person's religious background. I know it is now my time to bring the creative force of writing books to the seekers of Truth. I move me out of my way, out of my comfort zone and bring forth a spiritual work for those who desire to seize the moment and claim their entitlement to write books with the *Infinite Spirit*. I, Carol Batey, am a channel of good for spiritual writing to come through for my readers. I give thanks to you, dear reader and writer.

> "All of us need to find a way into silence, which allows us to deepen our awareness of the Divine."
> - Traditional Quakers Proverb

Do you have a "sacred space" in your office, home, business or yard? Do you have a place where you meet your God and write your projects? Can you start creating one this day? Can you make a commitment? If you don't have one, identify a special place where you can meet your Infinite Spirit daily or often.

Next, have you created your "spiritual practice?" My spiritual practice consists of silence, meditation and prayer, going to a center for worship, eating wholesome foods, reading uplifting books and materials, watching programs that are inspiring, journaling, doing physical work for my body temple and any good thing I would like to do. While I am still in bed and awake, I say an affirmation that I have prosperity, abundance, success, health and happiness in my life. An affirmation is a true statement that is positive about you or something you desire to achieve. Then, I implement The Twelve Powers meditation of connecting into my center of powers. Unity co-founder, Charles Fillmore, discovered this truthful technique after meditating on the clarity of each center. For instance, this morning my focus was for activation of all twelve powers: Activation of Faith, Love, Strength, Wisdom, Power, Imagination, Understanding, Will, Order, Zeal, Renunciation, and Life. Simply going to each power center within my mind's eye and calling them alive. Today my focus is on Spiritual Understanding which is located at the hairline of the forehead, and the corresponding color is gold. The color is symbolic and it carries active vibratory energy. The power of Spiritual Understanding, once activated, helps my ability to know God and know how I should go about doing the sacred writings for others and myself. I will share more on the subject of The Twelve Powers of Man and Woman later within this book.

Carol's Personal Mission to You

As a dedication, I love writing in the hour of 2 a.m. for you, dearest reader. To accomplish this 2 a.m. task, I must go to bed by 6:30 p.m. This gives me great joy. Right now, I am finished and this time works for me after my mind has rested. The soft music will be turned off. The lights will be turned off and I am going back to bed. It is now 5 a.m.

It's another day. I awoke at 2:30 a.m. It's now 3:00 a.m., Sunday morning. I am up writing. I am up writing to you, dear writer even though I wanted to wait till later. Be that as it may, I could not leave this sacred writing alone and go back to bed just yet. There were additional promptings that occurred all day long and now are added into this introduction for your spiritual understanding. You are reading about my process of developing my books and how I start. The book process before has followed this spiritual writing path. You don't have to follow my path; make adjustments for your own writing path. Follow a writing path that works for you. Each person must develop their own writing process and style.

Everyone has different learning styles and working structures. I can listen with my inner ears to the prompting, as well as I can see with my inner eyes and senses. Can you? This day, again, I am asking you to make a dedicated commitment to a "spiritual practice." You would not be here, reading this timely message, if you were not a "seeker" of a higher consciousness living as a creative writer. As I wrote before, it doesn't matter if you write non-fiction or fiction. It's all channeled through; you're the vessel for your soul. Become a clear channel for good to help another person on this Earth. At the same time, draw nearer to the Infinite Spirit as you learn to attune your spiritual ears and eyes to the heavenly promptings. Know and understand that your book is already done; it is written. It was created and written long before you came into this body; know this truth. Be still and know. Can you, my dear, be still? "Be still, and know that I AM God?" (Psalms 46:10; KJV) You too, are god made in the image and likeness. (John 10:34 and Ps

Writing with the *Infinite Spirit*

"If any of you lacks wisdom, let him ask God who gives to all men generously and without reproaching."
- James 1:5; KJV

As a teacher and book writing coach for others, the one question that I am asked most in a class setting is, "How do you write your projects with the Infinite Spirit?" While many people think that, as a book writing coach, I edit and fix other writers' grammar, this is not what I do. It not my aspiration to do any edits or to fix sentence structures. In my workshops, I am actually an idea person who helps others know which way they need to go with their writing project. One should understand their personal mission as a writer. The other mission I have is to inspire others to unlock their potential to write their projects.

The next inquiry is, "Should I ask the *Infinite Spirit* to assist me to write?" This query has been asked of me in various places such as churches, bookstores, classes taught, and via phone, email and other connections. What better deity to ask for assistance with a writing project? What so many people don't know and understand is that there are countless, invisible non-physical helpers; not just one or two. Maybe students are uncertain of the *Infinite Spirit* and its immeasurable role in our human lives. In our lives, we have unlimited infinite possibilities given to us through a thin veil that simply works for us. Jesus Christ used this vast power within His ministries. Others such as Sri Gyanamata, William Butler Yeats, Rosemary Brown, James Merrill, John B. Newbrough, Charles Fillmore, Emma Curtis Hopkins and many other sages who are here on Earth now, and others who have gone on before us, used this unbound power. Many then, and presently, refer to this daily living awareness as a Mystic Consciousness. In *The Revealing Word* (2010) author Charles Fillmore, one the greatest Mystics of this era, defines the word Infinite as: "The totality of Being including all knowledge, all space, all life; the complete all. Without end or limitation. It is which is boundless, immeasurable, and inexhaustible. God is infinite and eternal."

In the book, Spirit is defined as, "God as the moving force in the universe; Principle as the breath of life in all creation; the principle of life; creative intelligence and life."

Once this knowledge of Truth is understood properly and applied, one can write with the boundless Infinite Spirit in full confidence in a stillness of space, sounds and time. The word Truth is a Spiritual Law of Expression. When I say that you and I are prolific writers, indeed I am and you are. This is true for me, and I am expressing my truthfulness of who I am as a writer. When I say that *Infinite Spirit* knows all Truth, this is correctly phrased--this is a Spiritual Law. Ask the *Infinite Spirit* to direct, guide, speak to you, write through you and be ever so present for your book writing project before you start. Then give thanks! One can write with a confidence that powerful energies of wisdom, knowledge and insights are being directed into their Spirit from the Absolute Power of the Universal Mind; a Creative Medium. One must be open and receptive to the Divine impartations given from the Creative Medium; the Universal Mind. Creative Intelligence and Medium doesn't flow in an extreme way. It comes often as the still, small voice within your soul.

The time is now for you, dear writer, to bring forth your marvelous work; move yourself out of the way (ego). You say, "Carol what do you mean by ego?" The word ego is used often by many. In the Greek language, ego means "I." In the English use, it means "self." When I am trying to finish a chapter, I simply surrender to the writing process and become empty of myself (me and my ego) and let the words come through my soul. You were born at this time to raise a spiritual consciousness to a world that waits for your inspired works. It doesn't matter if the works are non-fiction or fiction. The audience who will read your works, either non-fiction or fiction, await the project's birthing. You are their teacher. Show up and produce an artistic, literary work for their souls to be fed. Why are you keeping the world waiting? Remove your questioning and show them the way or inspire their paths. Just be assured that the work for you to do is followed by those assistants on the other side; I can't stress this enough.

Developing a Spiritual Practice

In solitude a writer may put their "spiritual practice" into action and carry it out daily. As a writer becomes attuned to the promptings of the Infinite Spirit's nudging for them to write, record, paint or pursue any artistic venture, they may be prompted to write a statement that is unclear. Nonetheless, it came into their mind to write or produce messages, yet you will not be able to write down all the messages that are given to you. One must completely trust the spiritual process and trust in a Higher Power bigger than you. Enter into a silence; stop and ponder statements written for wisdom and spiritual understanding. Then my dears, one may receive an "A-ha! Moment" The author's mind may become quickened in the silence to the concept as truth. Often, the minds and bodies of poets, journalists, novelists, authors and playwrights are being used to create a channel of good by the *Infinite Spirit*. Charles Fillmore said, "Once the truth within us is received, our conscious mind and super conscious mind are blended, and spiritual energies are created into our soul and body. Then renewed power to express and write Truth is created."

In my classes, I share this insightful direction from Fillmore: "When entering the Silence, close the eyes and ears to the without. Go to (Divine Mind) within (consciousness) and hold the mind steadily on the word until that word illuminates the whole inner consciousness."

My Own Experience

My experience, on many occasions, is waking to write around 2 a.m. Yes, I am always sleepy. However, I know this is my appointed time to make contact with the Infinite Spirit to write. I am a willing vessel for the *Infinite Spirit*. It is my quest to say, "YES" and surrender. I enter into a silence and afterwards, I write; not clearly understanding what was written. Later, I enter another stillness to ponder what was given to me. Then, spiritual understanding is attained and a peaceful, joyful assurance is reached within me. Once the spiritual understanding is gained, then it is time to apply it into my life, world and affairs by using wisdom. Then, I share the writings with others. A writer, after achieving quietness will intuitively and clearly see into the subject they did not understand; as I did. Most often, in the quite moment I may receive more information and a bigger picture of the situation that I can image.

Spirit works like a movie projector transmitting images and thoughts into our minds, hearts and Spirit. If we don't change the channel of our minds, the rest of the movie will be created and the next scene. Subsequently, if the writer shares the information too quickly with another person, they may experience interference. When a storm happens, often lightning can intercept radio waves and the signal can get lost or interrupted. Your work can act in the same manner if you tell another person about your writing project to soon. We must learn to keep our mouths shut while creating our writing projects. You will know when to speak to another about this precious new adventure. It is up to us to seize the moments, and act quickly and wisely to produce interesting inspiration for others to see. Then, we must give thanks for the spiritual insights given to us and that more insights will come.

Inspiration Given

In your heart, dear writer, declare that a special reader will read what you have written. At that time, spiritual solutions and enlightenment will be gained, as well as encouragement for their personal challenges. This process is called setting your intentions for your book for reaching your readership. By setting your intentions, you are adding special attention to your written work and the reader will enjoy and become inspired. Don't rush the process of attuning yourself with the Infinite Spirit. If you don't have this in place quite yet, develop a "spiritual practice" of silence, meditation, prayer and a mantra of "I can do this project." Invite and extend the invitation for the invisible non-physical assistance to show up and help you. After calling the helpers into your writing project give thanks. Don't over analyze the process; just be married to your commitment and dedication to develop your quiet time.

    Your first intention is to be open to the influence of the *Infinite Spirit* and not have a closed mind-set. Start this practice for at least 20 minutes a day and build up to more time. Check out and read good books, watch uplifting programs regularly on television, do research on the internet or in the public library, take time writing in your personal soul journal, watch or listen to internet TV, listen to the radio, attend a center for worship, get body work such as Reiki, massages, reflexology and healing touch, eat wholesome foods and exercise. You may want to incorporate other positive actions into this practice. Don't forget, dear writer, to invite and extend the invitation for the invisible helpers to show up as you seek the silence. When you enter into the silence, think of nothing while meditating. Focus on nothing, and give up the time, give up your desires and need to control the outcome, thought and space. Once you come out of your meditation, give an affirmation of thanks for all desires being taken care of in your life. Everything you know is in Divine Order.

Silence, Meditation, Prayer and Mantra

    Whenever I mention the word silence or meditation, students say, "I can't enter that action." This is when excuses are being made long before silence or meditation is in practice. Dear writer, I would like you to at least embrace this concept for twenty minutes a day, if this is new to you. Just focus on your in going and out going breath and just become still. Once you focus on your breathing, thoughts of this or that will just go away.

This is what I do. I close my eyes and take deep breath blowing up my stomach area and the breathing within my nose and then allowing the air to flow out my mouth and letting the air go flat in my stomach area. This is really simple to me; it helps me to forget about everything. See if this enhances your writing. By practicing this simple act before writing it helps clear away the thoughts of what am I going to write? I feel calmer and you will too! It is not 1:30 a.m. I am up doing the revisions suggested by the literary agent which are necessary to make the book readable for you, dear reader. I have a full –time job working for myself as a massage therapist so I must make the time to complete my new rewrites of this book, which is another whole process.

My best work is done in the middle of the night and early morning when all things outside are still and quiet. This time works best for me because I am self-employed, but honestly you have to works out the time for yourself through prayer. Ask your non-physical guides what would suit you best. Before I retire at night I asked my personal angels and non-physical helpers to awaken me to work on this book writing project. I have a cup of ginkgo tea for memory clarity and alertness. Prayers and petitions have been offered to the non-physical beings that assist me this morning and I await there heavenly presence. I know and believe that my writing is enhanced and clearer after this prayer of desire and I give thanks.

As you read, the silence or meditation I am speaking of metaphysically means to have an empty mind. Think of nothing. Take the focus off of "I need words to put on paper." Let go and release all things you feel are of importance. Move you out of the way so that you can be a spiritual vessel. We are using the metaphysical realm of meditation as a pure thought to make contact with the Infinite Spirit's Mind. At this point, you could create a mantra to say, for example: In the book of John in the New Testament, the writer uses this positive, powerful statement over and over, "In the beginning was The Word." (1 John 1:1; KJV) When John uses this mantra, it transmits a physical vibration and becomes a sacred word for calming and healing. Ordinary people have also repeated an energy sound or phrase from a song, hymn or a tune to calm their hearts and minds. For example, when you are in a conflict, saying, "Peace, be still" to yourself will instill peace within your soul.

    For those of the way-shower Jesus Christ, one may use the word Jesus. Devoted Catholics, for centuries, used the words Hail Mary or Ave Maria as they respectfully repeat the words. In India, Rama is so powerfully used that Mahatma Gandhi effectively used this sacred vibration and changed his life. Gandhi went from being a lawyer whose practice was not doing well to become a peaceful saint who won freedom for his beloved country without a gun, but all done in love. Rama means "to rejoice." Now Rama has become a tradition of many people around the globe who seek change in a positive way. You want to choose your own mantra; just start today. Try it for yourself. Mine is, "I am god." You can be god of your own life without imposing on God's power.

    When you come out of silent meditation, a deeper awareness may be reached. You have made contact with *Infinite Spirit*. For the writer, your answers of what is next to do may flow easily to your mind. You may get a prompting to call a certain person only to find answers to the very question you had. Meditation is the time for quieting the mind so that you, the writer, can make contact with the dwelling-God within your soul. The answers are all within you! Take the time to develop your quiet time before starting. Then, as you get the answers you sought (or maybe you didn't), give an affirmative thanks such as, 'I thank you, Infinite Spirit, for the guidance that is shown toward my project.' Know that inspiration will come to you very soon.

> "The mantra becomes one's staff of life and carries one through every ordeal. It is not repeated for the sake of repetition, but for the sake of purification, as an aid to effort. It is no empty repletion. For each repetition has a new meaning, carrying you nearer to God."
>
> \-   Mahatma Gandhi (1869-1948)

Write Your Inner Thoughts Here

_____
_____
_____
_____
_____
_____
_____
_____
_____
_____
_____
_____
_____
_____
_____
_____
_____
_____
_____
_____
_____
_____
_____
_____
_____
_____
_____
_____
_____

You have Guides and Teachers for Assistance
In the book, *The Seat of the Soul* (1990), Gary Zukav gives advice that every person on this Earth has a non-physical guide and a teacher. Even though this is a

truth, so many people believe we are all alone working on our projects or even feel they create on their own and they aren't co-creators! Guides and teachers are often non-physical beings that have been born before on this Earth, real--or not. This is not my expertise. However, through meditation I have tapped the ethers to understand who helps us to write and create our projects. Guides assigned to us are not teachers, but they are experts in a definite field from a past life. If you are a writer or have a project, you call and invite guides or teachers in to assist you. For instance, I know I have felt the Holy presence of many assisting my creativity. Some, I believe, are the same non-physical beings and some are new spiritual energy just for a new project. I believe I have the choice to call in what expertise I desire for the project for my understanding. These non-physical beings are up close and personal; these are teachers. They know us and often they feel very close to us. According to Zukav's book, "A nonphysical Teacher brings you ever closer to your soul." (p. 99)

    I resonated with Saint Teresa of Avila when I read her books. I know she is my teacher and also a guide; I call her into my writing world. I light a white candle to her when I write and see her in all white. I have pictures of her on my office walls. Her books are on my desk as well. She stands guard over my literary works and teachings. On numerous occasions, I've written about the day's events that have occurred and moved quickly and efficiently to write the lessons out on paper. I knew I had been guided to the right people and places. How about you? The assistance of the guide or teacher that is desired works through ranges of non-physical light that are much higher than our own. It is a communion of light messages between the non-physical begins and us. As non-physical beings are pure energy they can easily communicate with us with through thoughts, feelings, sound, smells and sense. But it is our job to become spirituality aware of their tappings, communications and nudging.

This information shared by these beings should be useful to any writer who wants to be attuned with the Infinite Spirit for writing. I can only give you what I have experienced and know. I have been researching this philosophical and overpowering metaphysical way of writing. Always remember that the *Infinite Spirit* is always there. Now begin your writing with the *Infinite Spirit*.

What are Your Sincere Inner Feelings about this Chapter?

Chapter 2

Let It Be

"When I find myself in trouble Mother Mary comes to me whispering words of wisdom; Let it Be."
-- John Lennon (1940-1980) and Paul McCartney (1942-present)

So often I write words on pages and do not know what is next. Have you ever experienced this? As I write, I have learned how to listen inwardly for direction and the words that float to my mind; I just "let it be." I sit in my chair at my desk and wait silently in the stillness for a nudging of which way I should write to you. Patience is forthcoming to me as I know I must be still and wait. This, dear writer, is what is needed for you to overcome your fears and develop your writing talent, your craft. Attuning yourself to the Infinite Spirit is the first and foremost thing needed. Just like a piano that is out of tune and needs to be fine-tuned, so it is with our minds. It's a mental development process and training. There is an old saying, "Practice makes perfect"; try it yourself. Be gentle on yourself as I have had to learn to be as a writer; just let it be.

Today, I just finished a workshop at the Unity New Thought Movement Church and the Community-at-large. A minister of a traditional Christian faith asked these questions, "How do you write a full page of words?" and "What if the words don't come. What do I do?" After explaining the answer so many times to him over the course of the day, I finally said to him in a loving manner, "This is the fourth time. I will attempt to show you to learn to trust the writing process." I told him, "Move yourself out of the way (ego), let go of anxieties, remove fear, doubt, and worry in the spiritual practice that you are going to create. The reason you are going to create the spiritual practice is so that you can made contact with the non-physical helpers and *Infinite Spirit.* They will show you the way for writing your project to go". As I continued to share with him, "Your book is already written in Spirit; the pages are already filled with words. Believe me". I suggested to him to align himself with the Infinite Spirit. Become a willing, spiritual vessel and "Let it be." My dear writers, we make the process harder than it is with all the fear, doubt and worries. Once we learn to surrender and let go of negative emotions and trust *Infinite Spirit*'s Divine timing, wisdom will flow out onto the pages. Words will, and do, come.

Listen and take in the advice from Ascending Master Paranahansa Yogannanda (1893-1952), "When centered in your true self, you do every task and enjoy all good things with the joy of God."

Once more I say, put a "spiritual practice" and a personal soul journal in place that can become a way of life for you; a way of connecting to Spirit. This will become, and develop into, a mystical experience as you become one with your God. This is a big theme throughout this book. Put a "spiritual practice" in place and carry the action out daily for better spiritual and personal development and enrichment of your writing.

If you dream while asleep, know that this is one path that opens the gates into your unconscious mind. The strange messages may be informative messages from another metaphysical language. However, dreams while you are asleep are a metaphysical language and are one way of communicating with *Infinite Spirit.* You can develop a lasting relationship with your dreams and *Infinite Spirit* as you trust the communication process. There are positive celestial beings in the spiritual realms of our mind that give us information that may be useful. Resistance can hinder our progress and our writing process. It has been said by Daniel, Wyllie and Ramer, authors of *Ask Your Angels* (1992), "The Archangel Michael is the guardian of dreamtime, so you may want to invoke his watchful presence." (p. 242)

Being a dreamer myself, I do believe that I get hidden miracle messages within my sleep time and I look forward to the illuminating presence of the celestial messengers of Infinite Spirit. Once the presence of angels has given me a message, I soul journal the dream. There is always a pencil and paper by my bed for this purpose. You may choose to use electronic recording devices as well. Just remember to soul journal as soon as you awake. What do you have by your bed right now?

You may wait to ask your non-physical celestial messengers for an interpretation. Become proactive and dedicated to learning all you can about your companionship with your angels. There is so much valuable information on the topic of angels. I advise you to seek additional information on the Heavenly Celestial Messengers of the *Infinite Spirit*. Invite the angels into your dream state while they work with your soul. Ask for protection and guidance while in the awakening affairs of your day; see a white light all around you that offers you protection. Let go of your inner judgments and then bless their participation with you. As I write, I see a while light of protection, which is the light of Infinite Sprit, beaming down into my soul all around my office. You too can see this protecting light. When I am working at my desk, I envision a white light surrounding myself, my room and my desk. It protects me from anything that may interfere with my writing. To me, it's a spiritual protection from all negative vibes and any lower energy. I am a healing body worker. I do massage and I touch different types of people daily, so I also see this light surrounding my massage clients for their highest good and for their healing. After each massage I wash my arms and hands with soap and sea salt to remove the other person's energy and to become neutral.

When I learn, I share it with my readers. As a writing teacher who learns from her students, when they raise questions and share inspired insights, I too become a student. As a student, I learn so much from them. We can all learn wisdom from the well-known 13th century Jewish sage Abraham Abulafia (1240-1291). He attained extreme forms of information from his mystical experiences as he wrote, "Now we are no longer separated from our source, and behold we are the source and the source is us. We are so intimately united with It; we cannot by any means be separated from It, for we are It."

It, dear writer, is realizing your Holy oneness with your God or Higher Power and realizing you will receive and achieve spiritual awareness. You will have all answers given unto you for your writing and new heights will be opened for your learning. Remain a student, as well as a teacher-writer. Edith Anne Ruth D'Evelyn, better known as Sri Gyananmata, lived during the years 1869-1951 and was a devout disciple of Paramahansa Yogananda, founder of Self-Realization Fellowship. "Gyanamata" is translated to mean "Mother of Wisdom." The first name she took, "Sri", means "respect". To a saintly person, "Sri," it means "Holy." Sri Gyananmata wrote each day of the month for the early publications for Self-Realization magazine and advised in her meditations, "I am keeping track of many things--of children, of food, of the telephone, of the doorbell.

Voices call my name all day long. Let my ears not be too dull to catch Thy whisper before I sleep at night."

As a spiritual writer of non-fiction or fiction, we all should apply this centering prayer before we retire at night. Remember what Yogananda said about every task. As you are so centered, my dear, into your (YOU) true self, "Enjoy all good things with the joy of GOD." Before I go to sleep at night, I try to mentally focus on my writing assignment for the next day in a prayerful way. So when I am so awaken, I am fresh, renewed and ready to commit to the next phase of the writing project.

Do you Need Answers and to be Assured?

When the well-known group, the Beatles, was recording the White Album, Paul McCartney said that he was fearful. He experienced artist anxieties and was full of doubts about his creativity. His mother, Mary McCartney, had died of cancer when he was 14-years-old. While the group was recording the album, his mother appeared to him in a dream. He told his mother of his recording fears. [As you can see, everyone has a human experience of the negative emotion fear!] She spoke back to him and said, "It will be alright, just let it be." When he awoke, he thought it was so nice visiting with her again. Paul's mother provided the inspiration for him and John Lennon to write the lyrics and music for the song "Let it Be."

Now we don't know if McCartney's mom was a non-physical teacher or a guide; however Paul received the message without questioning. He was upset over the recordings and how things were going. After leaving the recording studio, he went to sleep and found comfort and assurance. How did he receive the message from his dead mother? He was open and receptive to the comfort of the inspired words of his dead mother. Paul could have said, like so many, "This was just a meaningless dream; that is all." He could have held on to the negative emotions and concerns about the recording. On the other hand, he could have consulted a Dream book, a specialist on dream interpreting or another person in the flesh. Ultimately, Paul respected and believed his inner feelings toward his dreams and so can you. One must believe that the dream has something important to say to you and one must be open and honest about their selves. Paul missed his Mother Mary's naturally instinctive side and nourishment that she gave him while on the Earth. Nonetheless, he believed her words and stepped forward into his destiny to create the song, Let it Be.

Over and over again, this profound song of inspiration has been sung and many have thought Paul's 'Mother Mary' to be the Blessed or Virgin Mary of the Catholic Church. This song was inspired by Paul's own mother Mary from the dream not the Virgin Mary who is an Ascending Master. Ascending Master's were men and women who walked this Earth as enlighten spiritual beings who transcended another plane in a spiritual transformation of consciousness from this physical Earth. These men and women gained mastery over their human life and having attained ascension they left this Earth and worked with certain humans to assist humanity's well-being in a supernatural way.

The entire song lyrics are so insightful, philosophical, thoughtful and overpowering I recommend that you look them up. Can you just let it be and let the message flow through you? As most of us know, dreams can provide reflective hidden meanings regarding our self-awareness, our healings, and our dark nights of the soul, our fears, our hate, our family, our career, our weighty emotions, our desires and our understanding, as was Paul's experience. It is up to us to go within and interpret the meaning given for us. The mind may send active messages to an unconscious, sleepy mind. If Paul had ignored his dream, he would have refused self-knowledge and inspiration that helped him remove inner conflict and tension. He was in a sea of doubt and the words were given, "And in my hour of darkness. She is standing right in front of me. Speaking words of wisdom "Let it Be."

How often can you recount a dead person you have known, perhaps a family member appearing in your dreams standing right in front of you or next to you; speaking words of wisdom? Your thoughts may be, "that's nice."You don't seize the moment. You continue the inner conflict of your shallow soul's yearning. Stop and ponder this. Maybe they were not standing in front of you, but near you. So many discount their dream experiences. So many people also say, "I don't remember my dreams" or "I never dream." Eric Ackroyd, author of *A Dictionary of Dream Symbols* (1993) writes, "Bragging about a lack of dreams is a sure sign that the person is hiding his or her fears behind a foolish bravado, preferring to remain ignorant of his or her own neurotic hangs-ups. But ignorance is not bliss."

In his book, *God is a Verb* (1997), Rabbi David A. Cooper shares within his introduction information about who helps him to write and learn. "Most of these spiritual guides speak to me from other realms..." The guides are non-physical guides from another realm he's referring to. Can you open yourself to hear from your spiritual guides to write your books, too?

My Dream Experience

On one of my occasions, I was researching my family history. I was stuck in my research. I had done, humanly, all I thought I could do. So I surrendered into the process, released and let go. After a few days, I was still trying to locate the family records of my great, great grandmother Susie, the dates were around the late 1800s, but I fell into a sea of nothingness. Nothing was happening for me when I would search at the family history library. One night while trying to fall asleep, I believe I went into a light trance. Susie appeared to me in a dream. Nothing was said in the dream. I just received a strong, overwhelming feeling. Therefore, I simply asked her in an ecstasy of space what this information is. The thought came to me to write the Mississippi archives around the 1830s. I did and within one week, they sent me a letter requesting $6 for the family records. Therefore, I believed in the insightful process of asking for guidance if I didn't know what to do. It was done unto me because I believed. It will be done unto you as well according to what you believe; "According to your faith be it done unto you" (Matthew 9:29; KJV).

Another Occasion as a Writer

On another occasion, I dreamt that I was in a corner writing a book in a silent, remote area. At that time, I was in the process of moving to the country setting of Carrollton, Georgia. Once I arrived and settled, someone sent me a donation for my writing project. I then bought a desk and put it in the corner of the room where I could see nature and the pine trees out the window. This happened just like I had dreamt it. While living in that secluded, quiet, out-of-the-way place, I met Saint Teresa of Avila, Saint John of the Cross and many more sages in 2007. I was able to spend much time in silence, meditation and prayer. My soul was unrobed and at peace. Nonetheless, my process for that book was different than with any other book I had authored by that time. This project would become book number three. My main focus was to write newsletters for my website every month. In turn, I would take those newsletters and expound on the writings. One year, I turned it into my third book which took eighteen months of extreme development. Before the book was completed, I dreamt about the cover. It had gold lettering and a white cover. While living in the remote place, every night I went to sleep, I would feel, and know, that someone was sitting on the bed.

On a different night, I had another vision while I was sleeping. I was caught up somewhere unknown to me in another realm. I assumed it could have been an inner realm paradise in the spiritual ethers. While asleep, unaware of the incident yet having a spiritual realization, I had that book in my hand and was shaking all over. Then, I woke up.

A dear friend shared with me, after hearing my dream state, that author Neale Donald Walsh has been said to have a similar experience. To my knowledge I have tried to find writing to confirm this action, but I haven't found it. Apostle Paul from the Holy Bible also had a spiritual realization of his oneness with Infinite Spirit. He wrote, "How that he was caught up to Paradise and heard unspeakable words, which it is not lawful for man to utter," which can be found in 2 Corinthians 12:4.

Charles Fillmore, co-founder of Unity movement, wrote in his book, Keep a True Lent (1999),

> This enter realm you will find the spiritual ethers heavily charged with ideas that turn to spiritual substance. As your consciousness (awareness) expands, you touch the everlasting truths and you find that every blessing is abundantly added. What seems new is but the unveiling of that which has been forever.

As aspiring writers, we make everything so challenging. We love to resist the unknown. Once we move ourselves out of the way, we learn to trust the process and the vibes given unto us as words comes through us. There is only one Power and Source of inspiration. Live so that you can readily tap into the inner realms of the Infinite Spirit.

When I teach, I love using music that corresponds to my teaching. There is a powerful Tapping song by Dr. Rickie Byars Beckwith. One line goes, "You are tapping on my head. Must be something I am doing right. But more than I need to know. More than I need to write."
How many times have you been tapped by unseen non-physical beings and the time was for you to write?

Automatic Hand Writing

The action of automatic hand writing is thought of when one's pen appears to be in the hand of a writer and it's moving without the person's awareness. Guess what, dear one? This also can be done by training one's self to use a personal computer or smart phone! I just don't have to use a pen or pencil I can use my laptop computer! When typing on a personal computer it becomes easier because you can use spell check to check the words. The writer may not be directing the pen or computer, but an invisible Spirit may be assisting. Automatic Hand Writing (AHW) may be portrayed as Spirit writing, autography, or psychographic. I know for a fact this has happened to me on more than one occasion of my book writing. Please keep an open mind and heart to this chapter and this particular informative information. Another word of knowledge, a person guided through AHW may be totally conscious; not in a trance. There are so many gifts of the Infinite Spirit. Messages can come many ways such as to the ears, eyes, smell, taste, hand movement, dance, art and just to our brain so that we know what is going on.

When I wrote my first book, *Parents Are Lifesavers* (1996), it was channeled by the *Infinite Spirit*. At that time, while writing the book I had no idea of channeling or AHW. I just knew of *Infinite Spirit*, angels and ancestors helping me to write. Two weeks after the manuscript was completed and turned in, the editor assigned to me from California called with concerns. I lived in Tennessee and the publisher was unaware of the media attention I was receiving. She asked about my personal connection to Parental Involvement. I had been on television and in the local media in my hometown every month. The publishing company had sent my finished manuscript to an education professor in my hometown. He called my editor and told her that my personal story was missing.

The publishing company wanted to know what the personal story was about. When I told them, they told me to write it. Within a couple of nights, I was tapped on the shoulder, no one was present and voices said get up and write the story. I was so sleepy. It was 12 a.m. I didn't own a personal computer and I hand wrote for twelve hours, every word until 12 p.m. and then my hand went limp. That was my first conscious awareness of the use of the paranormal gift of automatic hand writing. This was my first experience of writing a book. I kept journals. However, when I was in the process, I was unconscious of the energy of Spirit guides or teachers assisting me. I thought I was losing my mind writing for so long with a pen.

As I voiced my intention, now to finish this task I had been given, I know at the present time to thank my guides and teachers for the assistance given unto me. Of my own, I can do nothing. With Infinite Wisdom, all things are possible, if you believe. What do you believe my dear writer?

Just like now. It is 2 in the morning and my hands are starting to ache. I have been up now since 11 p.m. Plus, I wrote for 3 hours before I retired to bed at 9 p.m. I awoke to finish this work. I am not done now; nonetheless, I must retire to bed. Here is a poem that a dear friend wrote for your enjoyment:

A Divine Instrument
My hand moves across the page
guided by a force
an impulse outside of myself.

I can feel a subtle flow
from my crown
down my arm
to my hand.

This pure, intelligent knowingness
speaks into my mind;
informs my hand.

I watch awestruck
in virtual disbelief.

My Self watches as this body
obeys this energy from outside itself.

Peace flows along with the words.
A gentle, coolness fills my chest
soothing me
dissolving apprehension.

So I trust
yielding my hand to the One
that created it.

And then just as gently as it began
it ceased.

Like a slippery fish
the energy flitted away
leaving me quietly euphoric
wondering when again
it will take my hand.

Evelyn Bourne © Copyright 2011

As we close remember, my dear, it is the Father within that does all the inner and outer work for your books.

"Believest thou not that I am in the Father and the Father in me?"
- John 14:10 (KJV)

Chapter 3

Staying in the Writing Zone

"Deep desire is essential for spiritual growth."
-Charles Fillmore (1876-1948)

In the last two chapters you learned "how and why one should start" an intimacy with their Source, the Infinite Spirit. Now it's time to step into the writing work and trust the process of writing. I will give you clear directions; a step-by-step plan of action that you can adopt and change for yourself. Can you learn to dance and write at the same time? Play and listen to the Invisible Spirits that will, and do, help your writing? Today, my dears, as I write this message of inspiration and direction to you, I have prepared myself first. When I am in the writing zone I usually don't eat any food until I finish my craft. This works for me. I am telling you dear writer, to choose this particular writing process. I abstain from eating food for least the time period of my writing only drinking herbal teas, smoothies, water or fresh vegetable juices. Spiritually, my thoughts go inward to you to give you the important steps needed for you to make contact with the *Infinite Spirit*. After saying my prayers of thanksgiving for a wonderful and joyful day, I then repeat my affirmation; I am a wonderful writer which is a positive truth for what I desire for this day as a writer. This is my divine purpose at this time. I head off to the gym. Oh yeah, I fixed a blueberry smoothie, took my vitamins and herbs, and then left. I also brewed me some hot herbal tea, Calendula and Gota Kola, to take with me. Calendula gives a boost to the spiritual side of your body. The herb helps increase psychic awareness. Gota Kola, used in India, wakes up the brain allowing for thoughts to flow readily and lets words flow better for me. As I returned from the gym, it's now 9:40 a.m. Time for fun and playing in the sun. Later, it is lunch time and now naptime at 1 p.m.

Time to Get Down to Writing

There are so many family distractions of death, sickness, elder-care and disease going on in my family life right now. Distractions will come; that is a part of this life. Just know within your soul that all things will work for your good and that all things are in Divine Order. Go within your soul, call in and ask the *Infinite Spirit* to bring Divine Order for you when you experience these times, and you will. One must find inner balance, activate their faith and trust that process. I must apply my mental skill to an endurance of focus to my writing task. Expectations of others come into play with the family crisis of how others would like you to react and endure. Everyone is different and has a right to feel and act the way they must. This for me right now, includes my adult children's concerns about what is happening, and how others think about a person showing up at the hospital, nursing homes or a family member's home. I have a lot of family responsibilities. I have a step-father that I take care of in a nursing home. I have six adult children and my own life.

I thank God for the teaching of Spiritual Metaphysics that I have embraced. I have had to learn to release, let go and do what is only "mine to do" on this Earth. It is my understanding that I have a right to be, do all that I want to and have all I desire in my life. Thank God for the prayers for healing, the art of forgiving and loving and serenity. This work of creative, expressive writing has given me an inner peace; my purpose is a blessed assurance. It's my appointed time to write to you at 3:45 p.m. I see a white light around me coming from my head down to my feet. All in front of me is a white light of energy protection. This is time for silence; a quiet time from the internal chatter. A A time to see a clear picture of what I desire to create. A time to internalized a connection with the *Infinite Spirit* and meditation; this is a different time for me! It's been stated by Francis Lord (N.D.), "We say an artist 'creates' a picture; he really externalizes an idea." Being a visual artist and writer at that same time, I am blessed with having creative outlets. So many expressions come into play within my soul while on this life journey. My ideas and concepts are formed inside my soul and then created as a visual art of expression or put on paper for you, my dear, to read.

Desiring an intuitive empowerment so I may be in tune with the hunches, feelings, senses, telepathy, sounds, colors and messages being given unto my soul, and in this meditation, I am becoming open and receptive to receive an increased awareness of communication and skills from the Infinite Spirit. For that, I am grateful. As part of my spiritual practice, I evoke and invite the Archangel Gabriel, the protector of emotions, energies of arts and helpful creator. Gabriel assists all writers and journalist in communicating with others. I see the color red. In the Holy Bible, Daniel 8:15-26, 9:20-2; KJV, the angel Gabriel helps enhance Daniel's skills and understanding. I too seek this. It is also known that the angel Gabriel brought the information to Mohammad to write the Qur'an.

Tools for Enhancing Your Writing

After, I seek non-physical angels, animals, and teachers and the Holy Spirit for Divine assistance with this project of communication with you. Knowing I must invite guides into my life, world, and affairs, I am asking and have extended the request for Divine assistance. I call them forth. The non-physical helpers are given unto us to enhance our work, give us information about the healing of our bodies and change our belief systems.

    However, there are many tools that can enhance our soul to receive inspiration for the literary project. Here are few of my tools for this day of writing. I remember that, "Of my own, I can do nothing…." I open the windows and light clove incense in order to increase the spirituality within my home. I take a sea salt bath and burn white sage in every room and corner of my home. Many cultures, including Native American cultures, burn white sage. This herb is used to remove negativity and welcome a sense of positive peace. Healing practitioners use it to remove negativity and cleanse their space. It can also be used to fireproof a pot or burning bowl, abalone shell, fan or feather. Matches or a cigarette lighter will be needed. I am allergic to smoke; therefore, my ceiling fans are turned on as well. I use small amounts of sage to burn and open my windows for one hour, regardless of the season. While smudging, I take a paper fan to move from room to room, fanning the smoke into the desired area. I quiet my mind and see what I would like in my energetic space, within my home. The smoke takes away out the windows every negative thought and vibe. As I finish, my body's temple is smudged from the base pelvis to the top of my head. I know that my Spirit is strengthened and cleansed by my intentions. This ritual is done, intentions are set and I give thanks.

    My intention this day is to show you, dear writer, how to use additional tools to manifest your writing destiny! Metaphysical bookstores and health store may have the supplies. Today, I smudged around my doorways, windows, closets and my office clearing out negative vibrations and raising a level of peace, love and harmony into the sacred space. Afterwards, I felt mental and emotional clarity. My home felt light and peaceful.

At the metaphysical bookstore last night, I bought Psychic and Intuition natural oil; the scent is Jasmine, Peppermint, and Lemongrass oils. The purpose is to give a boost to your third eye which is located in between the brow. I choose to use this power oil in a burning set with a tea candle underneath. As called by the Hindu faith, Chakras, I anoint the 6th Chakra; my third eye and temples as I summon the non-physical helpers on the other side who assist my writing. I ask that my third eye and temples become opened to images and insights this day for writing. There are seven Chakras that run from the top of your head, the Crown, to the base of your spine, the Root or Base Chakra, within the body. Each is linked to a color. They are known as the energy centers of your astral body. These centers unite you to your Higher Self:

Red	1st Base	Spine
Orange	2nd Base	Sacral
Yellow	3rd Base	Solar Plexus
Green	4th Base	Heart
Blue	5th Base	Throat
Indigo	6th Base	Third Eye
Violet or White	7th Base	Crown

When beginning to set the stage or atmosphere for writing, tune into your body. See where you may have weakness according to this chart. Today, I want to improve my 6th Chakra, the third eye. Therefore, the focus is put into that area. I know that the 6th Chakra brings to my mind, soul and Spirit, insights, intuitive knowledge and spiritual senses; I raise the vibrations in that area. I see with my mind's eye the vibratory color Indigo as well in that area. In Chapter 6 of this book, I tell of healing a blockage experience I had with this particular area.

I know that while writing I desire an increase of spirituality and attunement to hear the invisible spirits. In the Shamanic cultures, power animal Spirit guides become spiritual friends to humans. Young men are sent out on a vision quest to find his power animal guide. The youth fasts and once that's completed, usually an animal appears to him. This often takes a while or the animal guides may appear later in a dream, vision or a live appearance. The power animal guide may be a small animal with a big message. However, they help one find their own authentic voice. The power is not measured by the size or strength.

Shamans are one the oldest healing tradition in the world from all regions of the Earth. Most are called by to be Shamans (practitioners or priest-like), by invisible spirits or through their family line. Equipped with many gifts, the one that stands out the most is their ability to live in two worlds: a physical world and a realm of a spiritual world. Being wonderful healers in this world, most go through many illnesses themselves only to find a cure that's given to them from the ethers, from spirits. This knowledge assists them as sacred healers on their Earthly journey. They are known as medicine men or women. Information is given to them mostly while in a trance. I share more in Chapter 6 on the topic.

I once went to a female Shaman, Karen Cressman, in my hometown who took me on a journey to discover my animal totem power. Her intentions were set to introduce me to my non-physical totem animal to me. The totem animal is the source of all shamanic power and the animal will always be at your side. The Shaman may use the journey to assist another's spiritual development, healing, information desired, psychological understanding, and connection with totem animals, guardian spirits or animals. The Shaman may leave their body as they journey to the unknown realms. Actually, there are no special skills required to tap into the hidden realms, just a set of intentions set for certain purposes. My purpose was to find out my totem animal. The process began and it worked. After the power animals are identified, one must research the animal who has given them the message. Mine is a wolf, which is a strong animal. The Shaman took me on a journey where she saw, heard and identified the non-physical beings. She told me that they wanted to communicate for my spiritual growth. Then, I started studying, on my own, their characters and wisdom. The messages were recorded on an MP3 recording device that I could listen to over and over again. One word she used in the journey was "source" for what the animal totems teach. The totem animals "source" me with information for my spiritual and personal journey. The idea is for those who know their power animal guide to use this information to bring them in touch with their own personal gifts and power. The messages the power animal guides provide are taught to us by the way the animal lives in their own habitat. They are our teachers. For instance, the wolf loves the active role of being a leader in the family, community, and also loves being alone; so do I! What this animal, the wolf, sources, shows or teaches me is how to work alone and receive messages to my soul. On the other hand, how to integrate myself in fellowship with others as a leader is how the wolf sources me as well. For my writing, I am alone most of my awakening time and I am very comfortable with that for I have wolf Spirit.

There are parallels between Power animal guides and the teachings of the Hindu Chakras and The Twelve Powers. These powers were developed by Unity co-founder Charles Fillmore, and consist of twelve power centers which are located from the base of the spine to the crown of the head. These centers give strength to men or women when activated. The following chart is adapted from *Spirit Animals and the Wheel of Life* (2000) by Hal Zina Bennett.

Chakra: Crown: Eagle
The eagle has the ability see the entire picture and what goes on within the Earth and the Spirit world. The eagle sees the big picture. When you are writing, especially about life-lessons, you want to be able to see the whole picture, not a portion.

Chakra: Brow: Mountain Lion
Open to life lessons from the elders. The mountain lion knows the difference between human and universal spiritual Truths. As a spiritual writer, remain open to spiritual Truths, so that you will not have to learn lessons over and over again.

Chakra: Throat: Personal Power Animal
This animal helps a person define and find their true voice. One discovers how to use their personal gifts of the Spirit by calling on their power animals. The Personal

Power Animal helps you to gain self-power, control over others; another having power over them; respecting the gifts with courage. When using this one learn to express your literary works whether it be non-fiction or fiction.

Chakra: Heart: Wolf
Learns how to love and care for others; Increase community and relationship awareness. Enjoy supporting others, being good to others and self at same time. Relate yourself to this animal that leads, serves and protects his pack and brings all information to his tribe and so can you!

Chakra: Solar Plexus: Bear
Increased awareness of self the Bear helps with. Allowing you to stand in your truth and individual power.The Bear helps you understand healthy boundaries of human knowing, humility and forgiveness. Learning to forgive yourself and your so called-limitations as a writer is first on the list.

Chakra: Hara: Badger
The Hara area help to you to take care of self needs; owning and steps into personal power. Exhibits healing care for its self and others. You will understand andknow a deep sense of spirituality. Develop a spiritual practice so that you will be taking care of you.

Chakra: Base: Mole
The Base helps you to Respect of the Earth. Recognizing the meaning of life and the Universal Source. Give back to others in writing good literary books or projects.

You are probably asking, "Carol, what do the animal Chakras have to do with writing books?" Remember, this chapter is about staying focused in the writing zone. The better equipped you are to bring forth your message, the more precise your message will be. I found this chart and adapted it so that you can see we all are one in this universe. We must merge our spirits with all things on this Earth. For example, I love the Chakra throat area's power animal. For this one, you bring your power animals into this area to use your true voice. Gaining self-control over your writing time, your life, world and affairs is a must. This is a wonderful tool to use here. You will be able to speak and write your truth of what you know and who you are. If you aren't aware of what your animal totem power may be, stay open. Close your eyes and relax see what animal comes into your mind. There are many Shamans living in the United States. Type the word 'Shaman' in a search engine for your area or go to a metaphysical bookstore and ask someone there if they know of a Shaman. My client, who is a Reiki Master, told me about her Shaman, whom I went to. The Reiki Master is an energy healer who has attained three healing attunement levels of Reiki--a non-invasive balanced healing treatment. She or he is able to pass this attunement on to others and teach them the process of assisting others' well-being. A Reiki Master passed the first degree to me and I am able to use Reiki now in the body work that I do. My desire is there, the respect for my clients is present as well, and I am totally inspired.

The Twelve Powers of Man/Woman

The Unity Movement's Classic Literary works of Charles Fillmore is *The Twelve Powers of Man*, I am adding *(Woman)* (1930). Fillmore discovered the tools of twelve inner powers and wrote about them in his book *Christian Healing* (1909.) At that time, the correlation of the energy power centers had not been completed in a book form. According to the New Thought mystic Fillmore (1999), there are twelve great centers. Symbolically, twelve means "completion." He also links one of the Twelve Disciples of the New Testament to each power. As a writer, one may attain and desire to be closer to the Infinite Spirit and seek a Higher Consciousness, and it is clear that Fillmore must have been writing with the *Infinite Spirit*'s guidance to transmit the wonderful information he revealed. The writer's thoughts become trained in a positive manner and the thoughts are increased. One should also seek to be a willing Divine vessel for their writing. The writer's human conscious thoughts are sent down into the energy center of his/her body. Once that action occurs and stays, the *Infinite Spirit* gives life and power to express in a writer's life.

At first, as an aspiring writer, spiritual work done was personal. They answer the call to write or to do the work of the Spirit. They say, "YES" and surrender. As one connects, the work becomes larger into the Universe. Each one of the twelve powers has a spiritual function. They also represent the call of the Twelve Disciples. The "I AM the Christ" spirituality is located at the top of the head. It has to be noticed that this is where Jesus went to pray the mountain top. Here's another tool. You too should start at that point; your mountain top.

> "The subconscious realm in man has twelve great centers of action, with twelve presiding egos or identities."
> - Charles Fillmore

Here are the Twelve Powers pathway centers and their represented Apostles:

The Christ -- I AM - Crown of the Head

Faith	Blue	Middle of brain	Peter
Strength	Light Green	Lower back	Andrew
Wisdom	Yellow	Solar plexus	James, son of Zebedee
Love	Pink	Back of heart	John
Imagination	Purple	Between the eyes	Bartholomew
Power	Light Blue	The throat or root of tongue	Phillip
Understanding	Gold	Front brain (just below the hairline)	Thomas
Will	Silver	Center of the front brain	Matthew
Order	Hunter Green	Behind the navel	James, son of Alphaesus

Zeal	Orange	Back of the head/medulla	Simon
Renunciation/Elimination	Burnt Orange	End of spine	Thaddeus
Life	Red	Lower abdomen/generation center	Judas (replaced by Matthias)

Note: Other New thoughts teaching systems may alternate the order of the love and strength powers. The Universal Foundation for Better Living, founded by Dr. Johnnie Colemon, uses love as the second month, while Fillmore's Unity teachers use it as the third month.

Just like the Chakras which have associated vibratory colors, so do the Twelve Powers of Man (Woman). Many have different locations. You may call on one or more of these pathway centers to assist your writing journey. They are tools for adding power in your life. Many of the powers can overlap and work together. Today, I call on the power of Imagination which works well with the power of Faith. I use the power of Imagination as I form a mental picture of this chapter and bring into reality a conception. Then, as I believe, I exercise Faith. Jesus said, "According to your faith be it done unto you" (Matthew 9:29 RSV).

What do you believe about your writing journey right now? Ponder that statement. Dear Writer, one must rise above human limitations of the thoughts of lack and not enough. There are enough insights, wisdom, and spiritual gifts to assist your writing task. If you can couple a few of the points in the body for combined assistance to help keep your focus, I know it will work for you. Do you believe?

> "And the Lord answered me, Write the vision, and make it plain on tablet."
> - Habakkuk 2:2; RSV

Dear Writer, I pick a tool; a power from the discovery of Fillmore and focus on that area. Within my body I see the area where I wish to increase spiritual power from one of the twelve centers. I pray for that tool or power to uplift me while writing and strengthen my mind, too.

Infinite Spirit did not leave us comfortless on this writing path; we have many ways to create the best projects. But we must be attuned, open and receptive to the Spirit's promptings and callings. Pick a powerful tool from The Twelve Powers and apply it to your life and believe it when you act.

Below is an example where I incorporate the use of the Hindu chakras, animal totems, and The Twelve Powers when writing a project: Right now, at this moment, I ask that my crown chakra become opened to information from *Infinite Spirit*, so that all written communication is understood by you. My crown chakra is located at the very top of my head, as is yours. I envision the color of violet or white streaming unlimited knowledge, which is being poured into the crown of my head. You can too. I am sitting at my desk with my palms opened and my Spirit willing to receive all that the non-physical beings that are assisting me now at 2 a.m.

Within the animal chakra systems the Eagle is represented at the 7th chakra. The Eagle is able to see the entire big picture in an Earth and spiritual plane.

Within the Twelve Power, the top of the head, or crown, is the I AM consciousness of Christ. Here is where your higher-self and the Christ (the *Infinite Spirit*) meet and become one in body, mind and Spirit.

My power animal, the lone wolf, sources (or gives) me discernment and his gifts from the wild. As an alpha, the highest leader of the community of the pack, he commands respect and makes clear leadership decisions and brings his tenacious strengths back to the pack by generously teaching his pups and team. This is my spiritual mission at this time, to write and influence my readers in a positive way. This is the signature of the lone wolf leader, and I am shown this by studying his mannerisms. The lone wolf works alone often. But he also affectionately spreads his wisdom to his inner circle, the pack, with joy.

As I merge these powerful tools together for my inner guidance, I share my writing with you, dear reader. My writing mission this early morning becomes very clear right now, "I am here to direct your writing path as an author and spiritual teacher. To give you the insights and inspiration to push you to open yourself to new tools that will enhance your ability to unlock your skill and potential to write and, if possible, to publish your books."

Write Your Vision, Dear Writer. Will You?

_____
_____
_____
_____
_____
_____
_____

Have you written your mission statement, branding focus, affirmation for your writing career or purpose your vision? Please take the time to do so. This will help you stay on point. You are so wonderfully made, dear writer, as you learn about your spiritual self. There are many points for God to enter into you. Remember the Hindu faith calls them Chakras. I have given you three ways: The Twelve Powers of Man or Woman, Animal Chakras and the Hindu Chakras systems. You can start to integrate the inner powers so you can enter into the realms and mind of the Infinite Spirit. God is waiting for you to write your purposes, my dear writer, to open up to the promptings and let the book and visions come through you. How willing are you?

You, the Prolific Writer

This is who you are; a prolific writer. That's what you are, my dears. I looked up the word "prolific" in *The New Webster's Thesaurus* (1996), to give you meanings of the word: creative, fertile, high-volume, productive and inexhaustible. This means you are a productive writer whose message will be delivered in a high-volume without losing your reader. You are an intellectual, spiritual writer who will produce good book projects in abundance. That's who I know you to be! Can you claim it? Do you get the picture of who you are? All power has been given unto you in heaven and Earth. As you tap into the I AM at the top of your crown chakra, your higher self--your spiritual self--will be united with the Christ consciousness. You are a spiritual being living a physical Earth experience. Never forget this! Step into it! Why don't you believe that you can bring that book to fruition?

You may be asking how I can use the working power of the Infinite Spirit to create books. As you write your projects, step into your destiny to write, apply faith and trust. Live your spiritual practice daily and you will be at one with the *Infinite Spirit*. With Persistent Meditation on who you are in relationship to the in-dwelling of the *Infinite Spirit*, you will gain confidence. As you gain confidence that you are in an oneness, your mind will be opened to receive the words to write. Use this scripture as a mantra this day, "Let the word of Christ dwell in you richly" (Colossians 3:16; KJV). Remember, dear one, that we all are the Christ, not just one person, but all. We can all reach that state of conscious enlightenment for our highest good. The Ascended Master Sri Swami Krishnanada has stated, "Empty thyself and I shall find thee." In reference to the Christ consciousness, I am not referring to the personality of Christ, but the enlightenment or higher consciousness. In every religion there is the higher consciousness, such as the God consciousness, the Buddha consciousness, and Krishna consciousness. In metaphysics, we believe that we all are the Christ, which is our highest good. So let the word (there is more than enough for you to write) dwell inside your soul. You just may want to just know that there is simply a higher consciousness state.

Open your Soul to the Wind or Spirit of Ruach
As you read this, have an open mind; pray for understanding. You are asking, "Carol what in the world is Ruach?" The word Ruach in Judaism means wind or Spirit. This is how consciousness and information are brought to the senses which are related to speech and emotions that are both moving freely within the body. In Judaism, spirituality is created upon Ruach level of soul.

It manifests when people are moved into emotions of tears when a poem is read, art is portrayed, a one has a glance of the natural world, or when one finds true love. They are moved by the Spirit of Ruach. Pray for the gift of Ruach. If the sense, understanding and purpose of life are deepening, the more Ruach is fed within. Everything is dependent on how one views their life, how they spend their time and then how they understand what they have seen or learned. The Spirit is affected by many qualities such as calm, relaxation, doubts, tension, fears and strength. When one's level of human consciousness is raised to a heightened experience, awareness is achieved or Ruach ha-kodesh, meaning Holy Spirit in Judaism. Once this all occurs within the writer, a Higher Self, your soul's energy or super-conscious mind and the Infinite Spirit takes over and transcends all boundaries and increases awareness. Then, the non-physical beings that assist the writer from other dimensions help give impressions to the writer's mind. The writer receives words and a book will unfold within one's soul.

      The book project is already done before it's even started; just call it forth. Go back into your mind as you are quiet and try to remember why you were sent to this Earthly realm to bring forth for others. This Ruach is a high aspiration to seek as one nourishes their spiritual practice daily; this will be attained. I just gave you the empowerment keys to successful writing. Think about it! Always see the protection of the white light above you entering the top of your head. As your mind is emptied and you connect to your Higher Self, the mind becomes trained to raise a higher vibration super-conscious mind. Ask for any information that is needed to write your projects. Seek any information about any personal issues that you may need to resolve so that your body, mind, soul and Spirit may keep the channels of communication opened and receptive by removing any obstacles.

Refining your ego is a must for transmuting an awakening for purposes of writing to others. Move "you" out of the way daily. One may need to forgive another person (release them and bless them), and themselves for any imperfection perceived as a stumbling block. However, be very specific when accessing fears, blocks, purposes, talents and skills perform a work of great writing. Release them and see them floating into a sea of nothingness in a big ocean. The negative vibes disappear into the void of nothing. Then, see the messengers of the *Infinite Spirit* coming to wrap their big wings of love and harmony around your body temple. Spirit guides will communicate telepathically; you are a spiritual vessel or channel. Receive the teeming information and give it unto this world. Everyone on this Earth who creates is used as a channel. Think of how your TV goes to a channel of your desire for your favorite programming. The signal and the screen are clear unless there is outside interruption. Nonetheless, you have to adjust the signal for it to remain clear. Your body and mind work just like that. They may need an adjustment.

Most writers and creative people connect with their spiritual guide and their Higher Self. They gain inner guidance and inspiration. Often this occurs when one is faced with an inner crisis. How many times have you needed spiritual guidance? This is followed by someone calling you with answers to your issues or maybe an impression popped into your mind. Your soul opened up after practicing your developing spiritual discipline. Therefore, you gained the needed intuitive insight. Spiritual guidance and empowerment is necessary to rid your soul of fear. This negative emotion will keep you from receiving information.

This afternoon I took a short nap. I am not sure if I entered into a daydream state which is another form of channeling. A person doesn't have to have a special ability to channel. The Infinite Spirit uses ordinary people most of the time that are willing. A person's mind, soul, and body just need to be relaxed and one must apply patience and practice. If you feel greed, a desire for material gain, selfishness and a large ego, then you aren't working in God's energy or the consciousness of the *Infinite Spirit*. Often, I feel my hands warming and tingling around the forehead, Third Eye area or Imagination. My mind is focused inward so that I can receive the messages, mostly when I am awake. I turn my head to the side so I can focus my inner listening.

Back to my brief nap: during moments of this sleepiness I saw a train scene of another time period. It was as if I was attending a movie and I heard voices speaking in the scene. Then, in another impression of my mind, I heard or sensed another person telling me to make sure I wrote the following activity for you. After that instruction, I woke up. I gave thanks. I thought I had only been asleep for thirty minutes, but the time was 1 p.m. Keeping my pen and paper by the bed, I quickly wrote my visual daydream or dream. My dear, remember to keep a pen and paper or electronic recording device by your place of resting or sleeping.

Step-by-Step
- Prepare yourself and home to become an open willing vessel for God. Say. "YES" to God and surrender and know like the Master teacher Jesus, "I and the Father are one" (John 10:30; KJV).

- Create your Spiritual Practice or personal soul journal with persistent meditations on the Truth of God's Word. This will open the mind to receive the working power of the Infinite Spirit. Before entering the silence, lay your issues before the *Infinite Spirit* in silence, mediation and prayer, exercising, eating wholesome foods, reading uplifting books, watching positive programs on the web and TV, writing your thoughts in a personal journal or on a personal computer every day. Then, for your book project make a commitment to write at least one hour a day, more if you can. Set the time aside.
- Lastly, if you lack faith to make demonstrations; which we do from time to time, carry this to the Father within (the center), in the Holy silence. "Ask, and it will be given unto you; seek and you will find; knock and it will be open unto you" (Matthew 7:7 KJV). After you enter into the silence, meditation and prayer, nothing is shown to you or nothing is felt. Give thanks anyway believing it will be done unto you. Be kind and gentle to yourself; just know that guidance will be given as you wait upon the Lord for information. All knowledge will be restored and all spiritual gifts will be added unto you, dear writer. Know that the task of the Infinite Spirit, selects, reveals, leads, teaches, comforts and searches for every human being who seeks this personal subsistence. This is revealed and received from the silence and mediation as one opens the mind.

I leave you these wise words from the lover of all of God's creatures, Italian mystic Saint Francis of Assisi (1181-1226). This practical man of God loved nature and the environment so much that he preached to big and little animals, ocean animals and mankind. Francis's major focus was placed on silence and solitude. He could not wait for that timely period of aloneness. Union with the Infinite Spirit depended on a "good prayer environment." He, like most mystics, made time for real solitudes to commune with God. Make time, my dear writer, for silence.

"In the same way he exhorted with the sincerest purity cornfields and vineyards, stone and forests and all the beautiful things of the field, fountains of water and the green things of the gardens, Earth and fire, air and winds, to love God and serve him."
-- *The Way of the Mystic*, Author Unknown (2005.)

Chapter 4

Welcome Success with the Help of the *Infinite Spirit*

"Success means we go to sleep at night knowing that our talents and abilities were used in a way that served others."
-Marianne Williamson (1953-)

Often, aspiring writers are fearful of tackling the barriers that they encounter when attempting to start their writing projects. One such barrier may be a lack of faith in their abilities to use personal computers. In order to overcome this barrier, I suggest that such authors invest in *Dragon Speak* (found on www.nuance.com/dragon/index.htm). This software allows the author to speak directly into a headset (sold separately) and then the software transcribes the author's words. See how easily that challenge was solved! Fear is often used as an excuse when one thinks that he or she might fail. Another barrier often encountered in an author's ability to follow through with his or her project. There are those writers who, often without knowing, obstruct the completion of their own projects by blocking the passage of information from their mind and soul.

I have students in my class who tell me that fear is a stronghold in their lives. Most of this fear is related to how these individuals were raised as children. Due to their inability to let go of this fear, they have allowed it to cripple their ability to become a successful author. These students, like many people, have carried their negative core belief systems within their souls. These beliefs are then manifested into their lives as negative thought patterns. A core belief system is a foundation set within our consciousnesses that we believe to be true about ourselves. Often, this foundation is created while young and then carries over into our adult lives. These core beliefs may, without your knowledge, control you and your life. Core beliefs are not always true and can be reversed.

For example, a person with a negative core belief system may tell himself: "I have always been told that I can never do anything right." Over and over, this person has reinforced this negative belief system with negative self-talk and, after a while, the person will begin to believe such statements.

When I wrote my first book in 1996, I didn't know that I had disembodied teachers helping me. I knew I had angels or the wisdom of the *Infinite Spirit* assisting me. I was clueless to the knowing of non-physical beings helping us humans. My path has been clearer since I learned this Truth. This is why I feel that this book is so important for you, my dear readers and potential writers. It was only by working with my inner voice that I discovered my non-physical guides and overcame my negative belief system to become the writer that I am today. You, too, can overcome your negative belief systems and become the writer that you desire to be.

My Students and I Share

The students in my writing classes have cried as they spoke of their fears, doubts and perceived limitations. One student shared that she just wanted to be invisible. As we listened to her try to express why she didn't want to be seen, I kept getting intuitive feelings that she had been abused as a child and was carrying these feelings into her adult life. It was clear that she didn't have a sense of self-worth. Yet, she has a book to write about the abuse within her marriage, another person owning her and other women's power. As her teacher, I want her to be successful in writing. I know that she has a wonderful message to give to women and men who are abused in their marriages or by their life partners. One thing that I am going to share with her next month is that I want her to unlock her potential to write her books. I would like her to read Saint Teresa's book *Interior Castle* (1946.)

  I, too, have experienced my own challenges in regard to my writing. I didn't believe that I had anything worthwhile or interesting to share. I didn't believe that my thoughts and stories would interest others. Then, I became aware of the negative core beliefs that dominated my consciousness. I often replayed negative comments said to me or negative situations in which I participated. By replaying these events and statements, I was reinforcing these negative messages within my soul and not allowing myself to make a fresh start.

  Once, I read the mystical masterpiece by my teacher Saint Teresa of Avila, which tells of her reasoning for not wanting to write her books, as well as telling of her unusual spiritual life. She was not like everyone else. Even her Bishops could not understand her spiritual and prayerful life. She became a successful author and business women even back in the sixteenth century, through her spiritual practices. To overcome her internal fears of success she turned inward, to her soul, in silence, meditation and prayer, listening to sermons, uplifting conversations, good company, spinning, attending worship, playing music, laughing and cooking, painting and singing with the choir. This list was adapted from her book as written by her, but translated by E. Allison Peers. Saint Teresa finally released her negative limiting belief in her middle age, around fifty. So did I. And, you can too!

Once I understood that my negative belief system did not have to define me, that I could rise above it and become a new person, I began to grow as a person and a writer. I had to let go of the negative beliefs that told me that I could never be a writer. I knew that I was being called to write books and, once I accepted that destiny and let go of the negativity within my soul, I was able to start fulfilling that destiny and bring my spiritual message to the world. Within my daily goings on, I had to engage in my spiritual practices daily to overcome my inner fears. So many people have the need to be right all the time. I didn't have to have all the answers for everything and I quickly learned it was okay.

No matter how many success affirmations I said, read or wrote, I found that it was very difficult to change the core beliefs that I were engrained in me during my childhood. First, I had to become aware of my core belief systems, what I was thinking and why I thought it. Once I had faced my inner demons of fear and self-doubt, I was able to begin writing my first book. During the writing process, I found that I was less fearful of failure. In order to face my own inner demons I spent two years working on my physical, emotional, mental and spiritual self. My goal was to become healthier, all the way around so as I lost physical weight. I also lost emotional toxins within my soul. Daily, I renewed my mind by changing my negative self-thoughts and replaced them with positive statements that I knew or wished to be true. I started affirming daily that the person I was while out in the world or in a relationship was the same person I was with the *Infinite Spirit*. Self-doubts I had about myself finally disappeared and didn't return because I understood and knew who I was in this world. Once I owned my truth of whom I was and why I was here on this Earth my spiritual and personal transformation began.

As an aspiring writer, I had to learn how to release my negative attitudes and emotions by laying down a false concept or idea each day and letting it float away. This process allowed me to overcome my negative core belief system and become less fearful. When my fear began to fall away, I was able to step into my destiny and remove the barriers that were stopping me from achieving my goals.

Using the inspiration and direction given to me by the Archangels, angels, non-physical teachers and guides, Ascending Masters and Power Totem Animals, I was able to remove the negative appearances of what I saw within myself and thoughts of my unknown fears and strengths. Often, we fear the unknown, but don't know what we are fearful of. With the help of Saint Teresa of Avila's books and the *Infinite Spirit*'s divine wisdom and guidance, I was able to learn how to move past my own self-imposed limitations. Once I moved past these limitations, I was able to take responsibility for my own actions, while allowing myself to become empowered. My Higher Power lent me strength so that I could become the person I desired to be. Yours can too, if you just listen to your inner voice and shed your fears and negative belief systems.

Carol's Prayer for Divine Guidance

The following is my writing prayer for Divine Guidance. My prayers are not the same everyday. This day, my intentions are set to communicate with the spiritual realm for advice on what to write and teach. I will open myself up to become a channel of good. A channel of good allows the highest good to flow through me as I write. I know that, even though I am on a personal computer, my guides, who are assisting me, will be able to guide my hands. While they tend to speak very quickly to my soul, I ask that they slow the thoughts and ideas down today so that I might better dictate their messages. Today, I am working on gaining a literary agent and making the revisions that the potential agent has suggested. Gaining an agent is a must in this business. I embrace the changes with joy. One can succeed without a literary agent, but it is my mission and call in this period of my life to work with one. And, you are reading the works that she critiqued and I revised. Developing and publishing books takes time, sometimes long periods of time. As many eyes look over your literary works you can not became doubtful and fearful of your self. This is a part of the writing process. I am writing this book for you gain a clearer understanding.

  This is the second day of writing. It is now 5 a.m. I am not going to the gym at this hour, as I normally due, because I have dedicated my morning to writing to you, my dear readers. I will go to the gym later today. I am adaptable. I light incense from India, known as Royal Champa. Many musicians burn this popular Indian fragrance at their concerts when they play live. Today, I am using this fragrance to attract good fortune to my home. It has the power to aid and stimulate healing, help a person overcome stress and uplift spirits. Try it for yourself and see what happens to you while you write. I have soft relaxing music playing in the background, but have not yet lit any candles.

  Here's my plan and prayers for this morning. I see a white light of protection in my office where I write. I envision this light as having been sent by the *Infinite*

Spirit and Archangel Michael, the protector of the Earth. I know that my writing partner is present: Saint Teresa from the sixteenth century. She has given me a clear insight in regard to my message to you, dear reader, on how to become a successful writer and overcome your inner fears. She wants us to know that if she could overcome her trials and tests of faith, so can you. This teacher has taught monks and nuns. Now, she will teach you and me from another plane. She says, "Read my books and understand what I have gone through the many 'dark nights of the soul' until Saint John of the Cross escaped from prison and became my confessor and shared with me what was going on with my soul. I went to Bishop after Bishop seeking an answer. There was none. I thought I was just crazy and depressed; therefore, I had nothing to give unto the world. I knew I had a calling to write, but I resisted my work for many years wanting others to do the work instead of me. I did do the work and my spirituality was heightened. I went on to make great strides in my spiritual journey as a business woman, reformer for convents, healers and teachers. I have been blessed to have been able to advise Kings and Queens, little me!" Her books are many. Here are a few: *The Way of Perfection* (1997), *Interior Castle* (1946), *Life of Saint Teresa of Jesus* (1991), and *The Book of her Life* (2008.) Her books were written about the late sixteen hundreds and were later translated by others in the nineteenth century.

    My eyes are closed as I enter into the silence and mediation that I need in order to make contact with the *Infinite Spirit*. I also extend an invitation to the Archangels Gabriel, Metatron and Uriel to assist me this day. These three Archangels help me with my writing projects and written communications. I call forth the

Ascending Master Thoth, the god from Egypt, who knows how to work the high magic of writing, music and the manifestations of anything needed. He has been known to heal and manifest with sounds, chants and tones. You can call on Thoth for inner knowledge. He helps me transcribe my inner knowledge into my writing. When you feel that you are blocked from your writing, ask Thoth to help unlock your potential to write your books. I have often asked this of him and will ask it of him again today. "I seek clear directions and magic to write this chapter." Then, I make sure to give him thanks.

The next Ascending Master I invoke is the goddess of arts and crafts and wisdom. Her name is Athena and she is from Greece. I usually call upon her when I am painting, cooking or crafting, but today, I need her intuitive knowledge and insights while I am writing. Writing is a craft that has to be cultivated, enlarged and improved upon so that communication can be correctly carried out. As I do the rewrites for this book, I place my abilities within her hands. I feel her presence right now.

My power animal, the leader of my path, is the lone wolf. He steps up to help me with the challenge that I face as I create and rewrite this book. He is loyal, knowledgeable and intelligent. The lone wolf gives me an inner ability to stay focused on this writing task without the praises of outside men or women. He is the ancient pathfinder and I seek his knowledge on this day. I know that he is with me right now as I look at his picture. His mystical, light brown eyes speak to my soul. He says, "Tell the writers that in order to dispel the illusion of doubts and what they think is the reality about writing, they need to start to believe in their literary works. Trust your inner guidance. You have the tools presented within this book; use them to build your inner confidence. You, as a writer, my dear, are adored by many non-physical friends and physical humans. Stay open and receptive to learning from Carol. We are using her as a clear channel by which to bring forth this timely message for you. The hour is nigh for us to provide you with this information. Now, you have it. You, aspiring writers, are often the greatest gift to your writing abilities, as well as the biggest block to your destiny. No one else can align your soul with the words that you need to share and no one else can keep you from sharing these words. Your spiritual practices may vary from those practices of others, but as long as you set aside time each day for silence, meditation, affirming prayer and journal writing, as well as eating wholesome foods, exercising, reading and listening to uplifting music, which will raise your inner vibrations so that you can hear your souls yearnings, you will have created a successful practice. Fear not, for we (the non-physical beings) are all with you. You must merely ask for our help." So be it!

I request that my Guardian angels watch over me as I communicate this message to you today, my loved ones. I need their help in order to allow the information within my mind and soul to correctly flow from me into this book so that it can be shared with you. I ask for a spiritual focus and tenacious Spirit, which the lone wolf has, in order to gain the will to teach, protect, live and give.

My 7th Crown Chakra is now activated and opened; the white light from the *Infinite Spirit* is being poured into my Crown Chakra as I seek additional spiritual knowledge and wisdom this day in regard to what to write to you. I accept this gift and writing manifestation. I know that the words are there and this work will bless the reader. I ask the *Infinite Spirit* to accept this generous offering of my affirmative prayer and writings for my readers. Amen

Can You Answer the Following Questions?

Take a few minutes to understand your core beliefs in regard to your writing projects. What emotions come to you when you think of writing? Take the time to write your feelings here. Do you feel fear, sadness, anger or guilt?

_____
_____
_____
_____
_____
_____
_____
_____
_____
_____
_____
_____
_____
_____
_____
_____
_____

When you think about writing, what is your greatest fear? I would like you to call on Archangel Uriel to help you to overcome your barriers to your writing talents. Write your prayer to Uriel here. Follow your prayer with your perspectives on your fears in regard to your writing projects.

Now, I would like you to write two things that you know you would be good at writing. These items may also be considered writing strengths and can include the ability to solve problems for others or a means by which to better understand yourself spiritually.

Examine your negative core beliefs and access what is keeping you from stepping into your writing destiny. Then, call upon the goddess Athena and ask her to unleash your creativity so that you can write your projects. She is waiting for you.

_____
_____
_____

Call on Your Non-physical Guides to Assist You

     My students are often afraid to start on their writing projects. They say the main reason they are afraid is that they feel overwhelmed. If you feel overwhelmed while working on a project, simply invite your non-physical beings to help you. Start with a desire and intention to write. Grab a pen and paper, your notebook, a personal computer or an electronic device. Start writing. Do not stop until you have an entire page of words.

     Desire means that you, very strongly, want to have something happen. Set your goal for your writing intentions. Create a plan for your project. Your goal could be to decide what you are going to write about or for whom your book will be written. If you feel blocked from writing, call upon your non-physical, disembodied guides. Ask them to assist you in removing this obstacle. Each of us has at least two non-physical guides assisting our writing projects. It doesn't matter if you know the names of these guides or just feel them. Simply believing in them is enough to entice them to help you. Can you believe? When you seek a direction for your writing project, make sure to call upon these guides.

     Many authors enter into a dreamlike state or trance when receiving information from their guides. Do not be alarmed if this happens to you. Other times, authors will find that they are not in charge of their voices and someone else is speaking through them. This other voice is also your guide. Do not fear if this happens.

Think of such instances as playing a part. You, much like an actor, are speaking the words of another, words that were meant to be expressed to the world. You are the vessel for this expression.

Ask your non-physical beings for organizational skills so that you can organize your writing in a manner that will benefit your readers. They may provide this knowledge to you in a variety of ways. They may send someone to you to answer your challenge or they may whisper the knowledge into your soul's ear. Either way, you must be ready to receive this knowledge. You must be tuned in to the world around you and open to receiving what will be given to you. Remember, once you ask for guidance, all you have to do is wait, and listen, and it will be provided to you.

Are you a People Pleaser?

Many artists, musicians, writers, actors and actresses are people pleasers. When you are a performer, often, deep down, you entered this occupation or hobby because you sought the approval of others. Within their core belief systems, these individuals often believe that they are nothing until they receive a pat on the back. Is this statement true for you? If so, you need to realize that only you and the *Infinite Spirit* need to be pleased with your actions. You answer to no one else. No one else's opinion matters.

Of course, such a response is easier written than done. It has taken me a lifetime to overcome my desire to please others. Often, I felt that I was not good enough or smart enough to please the others around me. These thoughts became a stumbling block for me. If I had not been able to overcome this desire to please and feelings of inadequacy, I would have never been able to succeed in my writing career.

Growing up, my core belief system told me that others were more important than me. Therefore, I never made a decision without getting someone else's approval first. One reason I felt this way was because I did not have a formal education. I chose not to go to a four year college, although family members have many degrees and formal education. Even though I knew that career educational path was not for me, I felt not unequal in my family structure because of the way my mother, and her siblings and mine, viewed a formal education.

When I was in my 30s, I realized that I had given my personal power away at an early age in order to please everyone else. I hadn't realized that I only needed to please myself and the *Infinite Spirit*. This lesson was a difficult one to learn, but I needed to learn it as my beliefs were hindering my spiritual and personal growth. There was no one to blame, but myself.

Once I learned to let go and only please myself and the *Infinite Spirit*, I began to bloom. I could make decisions without worrying about what others thought of them. I began to focus on my writing, uncaring of what others thought of my books or my desires.

However, I would still find myself saying, "I lack a formal education. I can't write." I had to learn to let this doubt disappear and, instead, open myself up to the tapping on my heart, tapping from my guides and the *Infinite Spirit*, telling me to follow my dreams and bring my spiritual and personal messages to my readers.

When I looked at my self-imposed limitations, I felt the desire to run, hide and dismiss the call to write. However, I chose to overcome these limitations and then opened myself up to those above me speaking the truth.

Within this truth, I found my own powers. After writing my third book, I became comfortable with myself as an author of spiritual messages and my connections with the Infinite Source.

"The human will has its limitations. So far and no farther says the law. The divine will has no limitation...The great secret of life and power, then, is to make and keep a conscious connection with this Infinite Source."
- Ralph Waldo Trine (1866-1958)

Do you feel comfortable in regard to your relationship with the *Infinite Spirit*? What has your voice told you about trying to please others? Have you found that you cannot achieve your goals due to your desire to please everyone else? Do you still try to please everyone else? Write your thoughts below.

_____
_____
_____
_____
_____
_____
_____
_____
_____
_____
_____
_____
_____
_____
_____
_____

Demands and Needs

Can you create a book or writing project based on the demands and needs of an audience? Each of my books has been developed from information that needed to be brought to this Earth. When I first started writing in 1984 (*Parents Are Lifesavers*), Corwin Press had their acquisition editor call me. They asked me to write a book based on a need that they saw within the market. I answered the literary call and provided them with the information that they desired. I had recently used the same information to help a school district in Nashville, TN.

In the early 1990s, while working at the Metropolitan Nashville Public School System, I felt that these ideas and concepts should be spread throughout the country. I had a vision that showed this need, but I was unsure how to follow through with it. At this time, I was not attending a New Thought Christian Church and knew nothing about the Law of Attraction. I just knew that I felt the pull of a call to move this idea into the national spotlight. I knew that teachers needed to understand how to move parents into the classroom and encourage them to help out at their children's schools.

I have learned many things about non-physical beings while on my path. I have learned that there are spiritual, non-physical beings, called angelic beings, who watch over this Earth and the cosmic planes to order to help raise our inner knowledge to a higher level of consciousness. They decide what we need to know in order to advance on our spiritual journeys. These angelic beings desire to bring such messages forth to others. They continually protect us from lower levels of negativity and provide us with heavenly guidance and inspire us to become our true selves. Other names for these beings are Truth teachers, Buddha, Jesus, Lady Nada, Mother Mary (Jesus Mother) and Melchizedek. It is my personal belief that my desire to serve and bring the Parent book into reality for the world was prompted by the Council on the other side in the spiritual realms. There are those who have ascended or left this Earth who assist us with heavenly knowledge here. They are often called the Great White Brotherhood or the Council of Light. In Doreen Virtue's book *Archangels and Ascending Masters* (2003), she give a definition in her glossary of terms: Leaders in Heaven who oversee the safely and spiritual direction of Earth and her inhabitants, and also the light-workers who help upon the Earth. This is not a reference of a race but the white lights that surrounds the members of the council.

    I am pleased to say that the above book is still selling after the many years. In fact, it is recommended reading for many student teachers at various universities. As such, I receive a royalty check once a year for this book. However, I do not own the rights to this book, the publisher does. I know that I was simply used as the channel through which this book was published. I was used in order for my guides to spread this message among parents and teachers in order to improve education within this country.

    You, too, can be used as a channel by which to bring forth an intuitive message to the world. You must simply open your mind, heart and soul to the prompting of the non-physical council.

    Anne Lamott, a novelist, writes non-fiction stories on depression, Christianity, alcoholism, single motherhood and laughter. She once wrote that she began to write these books because she enjoyed reading books that focused on real-life solutions to everyday living. Her books, which included information on spiritual transformations and humor, are presented in the form of memoirs. She has spent many years as a writing teacher and uses her books a means by which to heal her soul. *Within Hard Laugher* (1990), she provides advice on how to find your intuition: "You get your intuition back when you make space for it, when you stop the chattering of the rational mind."

Success as writer, my dears, is up to you and you alone. This craft must be refined and practiced daily. A writer must write something each day. What you write must simply come from your soul and you must not judge it. Simply learn how to be free to express whatever needs to be released from your soul. Refinement comes later. Seek guidance from your non-physical beings. They are here to help you! Deeply look at your limitations and find ways to overcome them: enroll in free basic computer courses at your local library, sign-up for a writing support group, seek online support in which you can share your writing with other aspiring authors. Don't ever let a "lack of education" stop your from moving forward in writing your projects. Ask for assistance from others who have the talents and skills that you sense you lack. I do daily! I will leave you with these powerful words from Ralph Waldo Trine,

> When one becomes thoroughly individualized they enter into the realm of all knowledge and wisdom, and to be individualized is to recognize no power outside of the Infinite Power that is at the back of all. When one recognizes this great fact and opens up to this Spirit of Infinite Wisdom, they then enter upon the road to the true education, and the mysteries that were closed

now reveal themselves to them. This must indeed be the foundation of all true education, this evolving from within, this evolving of what has been involved by Infinite Power.

Once you, dear writer, become one with the source of all knowledge and wisdom, you will know that nothing is greater than the power of the *Infinite Spirit*. This lesson is the most important of all. All knowledge and wisdom originates with the *Infinite Spirit*. It took me until I wrote my third book, *Poise for the Runway of Your Life* (2009), before I learned this knowledge. I hope that my message has helped you learn it sooner in your writing career.

Note from a Former Student
Why Aren't You Writing? An Aspiring Writer's Challenge to Unblocking Creativity

I have wanted to be a writer since I was 15-years-old and a sophomore in high school. I was inspired to pursue this calling when I won first place in our school's world peace essay contest. My essay focused on the fact that, for peace to be achieved in the world, we each must find peace within our own hearts. Our pastor asked me to deliver this message as a talk at our church during the Sunday morning service. Although I had a bit of stage fright, I found it exhilarating to know that he thought I had something of value to share with the congregation. This initial success was the beginning of my desire to write materials that could potentially help other people in their quest for spiritual growth. As with so many aspirations that come at such an early age, my goal of writing was pushed to the back burner when I left college and began working to "earn a living."

Fortunately, I landed a job in the media in my early 20s. I worked in this career for over 34 years, first as a television producer and later in an online publishing environment as a content manager, editorial director and executive producer of a major corporate website. In this career path, my time was primarily focused on hiring, training and managing a rather large staff within a fast-paced and competitive business environment. This was challenging, exciting and creative, but not conducive to having enough time to pursue my dream of writing articles and books with the theme of spiritual growth, as I had originally planned.

Last fall, my corporate media position was eliminated as part of a rather large downsizing. All of a sudden, I found myself with time to do the things I had always wanted to do -- exercise, meditate, spend time with friends and family, and, yes, I finally had time to write. What I didn't expect was to find that after all these years of stifling my desires to express myself through the written word, writing no longer came easily for me. I still had the desire to write, but I felt stuck and fearful that what I had to say had already been said by others, far more eloquently than I could ever say it. I knew enough about metaphysics to recognize this as FEAR (the acronym being false evidence appearing real). Plain and simple, I had to face it head-on and let this fear-based thought know that it had no power over me. But the questions that were foremost in my mind were, "Where do I begin?" and "What can I write that will make a difference and be helpful and meaningful to others?" I realized that I was afraid of looking foolish. I had worked with some of the best writers in the business. How could I possibly put my work out there for critical review? I completely shut down. I prayed diligently that the heavens would open up and give me the answers. There was a long dry spell that went on for several months -- though it seemed more like years.

In January of 2012, I went to church and noticed an announcement in the bulletin about a class that looked like an answer to my prayers. The class was called "Writing with the *Infinite Spirit*" and would be taught by Carol S. Batey, author of several books on a variety of topics, mostly spiritual in nature. The title of this seminar spoke to my soul, so I signed up immediately. I was hoping to get the answers that I had been seeking. I wasn't disappointed.

Prior to the class, Carol gave us the assignment to read her book *Why Aren't You Writing: Unlocking Your Potential to Write Books*. As I read, I began to realize that many writers felt the same way that I did at the beginning of their careers. In class, Carol suggested seeing our perceived obstacles as challenges rather than blocks to expressing our creativity. She offered a plan of action to jumpstart the creativity of aspiring writers. This plan consisted of a series of things that would serve as a preparation ritual for beginning the creative process. She advocated preparation of one's mind, heart and soul through prayer and meditation. She also recommended designating the space in which one would write and checking one's ego at the door before entering this sacred space. Carol states, "There are voices that push you along the way. As spiritual beings on this Earth, you will face adverse conditions on your path, but do not look at the situation as right or wrong. Look past the objection and see the outcome you want to achieve. It is our Earthly task to use our free will and discernment powers to move forward and not against the grain. Most problems are not as they appear."

Carol's voice is one that is serving that purpose for me. She has inspired me to look beyond the challenges and beliefs in fear, writer's block, or anything else that would prevent me from writing, and to accept the realization that we are all here for a higher purpose. Her message is that the *Infinite Spirit* speaks through those who genuinely offer their time and talent for the greater good. This guidance is readily available to unlock the joy and exhilaration of the creative process. Carol shares this information from her heart with passion and a sincere belief in its ability to change one's course. She does this effectively because she has lived it and has seen her dreams of becoming a writer come to fruition. In addition to offering ideas about meditatively preparing your heart and mind for the words to come through, she also advocates designating a regular time to write. Carol also shares her personal experiences about finding an agent, working with editors and publishing companies and discovering surprisingly easy and inexpensive ways to self-publish and market one's work. There was so much information packed into her four-hour seminar that I had to write quickly to make sure I didn't miss anything in my notes. Much of this information I had never heard before, and some I was hearing with a fresh perspective. Carol's approach to the process of writing began to give me hope that I could actually fulfill my lifelong dream to become a published writer. I began to get excited about writing again.

What comes next? I will simply do the next right thing, which will consist of rolling up my sleeves, invoking Spirit and remaining open and receptive to letting the words flow through me. As Carol says, "If you have a desire to write, your book is already written in the

infinite, you just have to be still and receptive and let it come through."
-- Donna Priesmeyer, Aspiring Author

Chapter 5

Personal Soul Journal

"Writing is the only thing that, when I'm doing it, I don't feel I should really be doing something else."
– Gloria Steinem (1934-present)

Tonight! Thursday, September 9, 2011. Silence is upon me for a moment. I invite the non-physical assistance to come in. I give thanks. I am now writing this at 7:30 p.m. A white candle is lit to welcome my writing partner, Saint Teresa, and the host of angels. Within my mind's eye, I see Saint Teresa in white; what a blessing. I welcome my animal Spirit's presence. The holy incense of lavender is being burnt in another room. Soft music is playing nearby. The scent of lavender may be used in a drawer; it produces relaxation and changes moods for the better. I like to pull the fresh leaves from an herbal garden and put them inside my pillow case. This aromatherapy was once used to tame tigers and lions. It has such a calming effect; it really works well on anxiety. The scent of lavender is a perfect fragrance to add to a bath or when retiring for bed.

Do you keep a personal soul journal? Create a daily journaling time that you can write your experiences, feelings or special events. Many people use journal writing to express their soul's fears, illnesses, mishaps, angry feelings, human weakness, as well as strengths. It's a time for their inner talk without judgments; just true reflections. Make the time, even if it's only 20 minutes a day. This is a time when your utmost secrets are shared with oneself. Most people who keep a personal soul journal write it at the same time every day. Can you set the same time aside to write your inner feelings? Do you have questions you wish to ask the Infinite Spirit? Listen carefully and intuitively in your inner conversation and be mindful of the still small voice within your mind. I love allowing a word from a spiritual minister, TV show or an email to prompt me further to write a paragraph on my life. Do you have a sacred place within your home that is dedicated to your spiritual advancement? Remember, don't judge your writing. Write in free styling, feel at ease and practice daily. This task is not about editing and sentence structure; it's about getting what's in your soul out on paper. You may get a spiral notebook and use it for a journal. Some use a diary or fancy journal purchased from store or online. The most important thing to do is to express your thoughts freely for inner emotional healing and opening up your soul. FREEDOM!

Try a Personal Soul Journal

Maybe you don't want to be published. Some of you just want to leave a legacy for your children. Legacy, to me, is a walk of a person's life on paper. Some of you may love the art of journal writing daily as a personal soul expression. A few may just want to publish memoirs for the family or of their family history. Then, there are those who want to get their messages out to the world. You might try blogging on the internet. A blog is free and it's another way to express your own personal thoughts on a certain subject and share it with others. I write for all of those reasons, so can you! Just make a weekly schedule to check in with your feelings and what's coming through and then blog it out!

In the Mormon religion, the members are encouraged to keep a personal soul journal for their family members and their children. Isn't it wonderful to see where a family member has been and how the Infinite Spirit has brought them through their personal trails, family and health challenges and strengths. Also, in the Mormon religion, the members are asked to do their personal family history; a genealogy. In most African-American families, family history is a real challenge. Without the use of computers, I was able to research my former husband's and my family back to slavery. By reaching out to the oldest members of the families and with prayer for guidance, I was able to get the information; the search was fulfilled. Nonetheless, it is my belief that the kinfolk who had gone on before me on the other side helped guide me to find the information. Therefore, you too can receive this kind of assistance if you are seeking family history. This will be the next information I give to my children when I sense they are ready for the files. One of my family members, who just found our family, the Madrys, now knows she has a family. In that case, my grandfather's brother got her mother pregnant while he was in the Navy. She went from California to Utah to the Mormon family history library to look up the Madry family files and found everyone. Thank God I had submitted the family's history to the Mormon genealogy archives in Utah. She now comes to all the family reunions and keeps in touch with family members. So, as a suggestion, you can also do family or business newsletters, text or social media, emails to get yourself writing. My family does all three to keep the family connected.

A Gift from Beyond

      When I was a child, I never knew my father, Fred Johnson. My mom used to say that I had Indian blood like him and I acted like him. He died when I was nineteen years old. Within my soul, I would wonder what she was talking about. Thank God, my mom would say those things to me! Therefore, I worked the information for my good. As my curiosity grew over the years, little did I know I would come to know him by research and word-of-mouth. Once I joined the Mormon Church at age twenty-eight, I did research on Fred and loved all the information I found. His second wife and his favorite cousin were still living. I went to both people to find out about my dad. The information was so freeing to me. The scripture states, "Then you will know the truth, and the truth will make you free" (John 8:32; NIV.) I found out that he was a compassionate man and very sensitive in nature. He was ½ Cherokee Indian and African American. I know, and feel, his presence with me when my heart is heavy and burdened down from life.

    In the Mormon religion, which I was a part of for about sixteen years, I kept a personal soul journal of my daughter Jai's adopted birth. I started keeping a personal soul journal when we joined the Mormon Church knowing we were in the process of adopting a child. I wanted our adopted child to have a legacy of hope and know how to endure life. I wrote to our child and to the Infinite Spirit. I made my request known to God. Later, after the adoption went through, I wrote to Jai, our adopted daughter, about the family's daily activities. When she turned thirty years old, I gave her the journal I had kept to keep for one year or so. She cried and cried. I wrote about the experiences in my fourth book *What's Cooking in Your Soul?* (2010).

    My writing style in my personal soul journal is very different from the writing here. No editing or spelling corrections; it's just a place where I felt safe to be a mom and a writer. It is still the same now in my personal soul journals; no editing or spelling just writing my expression. It's a time for my inner healing of my emotions and desires! I often use a spiral notebook.

Try Journaling Your Day Here

_____
_____
_____

How's your creativity? You may not realize that writing in a personal soul journal is a form of creative expression. Do you have repeated issues in your life that are weighing you down? Then, tap into your soul and journal about what you sense, real or unreal. Are you blocked from writing? Often, this is creativity on hold!

Do something outdoors or change your atmosphere and then come back to your writing. Check in with your emotions. What do you feel about this or that? Are you comparing yourself with others? Do you wish that you were somewhere else in life? My dear, count your blessing and name each, one by one, until your emotions change. Quiet your inner negative chatter; it blocks the writing flow of creativity. Change your thinking and outlook on life. WRITE IT OUT!

"Writing is a form of prayer."
– Franz Kafka (1883-1924)

Chapter 6

Desire, Expect, Believe

"Do you have the belief in you to move on, even when the whole world is against you, with swords in their hands?"
-- Swami Vivekananda (1863-1902)

Last night, September 8, 2011 at 6 pm, I went to a Reiki support group session for a "laying on hands healing and sound tuning." Religious cultures around the globe have practiced the gift of "laying on hands." When I was in the Mormon religion (The Church of Jesus Christ of Latter Day Saint), this symbolic act was carried out by men of its priesthood for counseling, sickness and to confer the Holy Ghost upon another. In the Jewish tradition the "laying of hands" has become a spiritual ritual called Tanakh. Kings during the period of the 16th Century in England and France healed skin disease with Divine Touch.

In the support group, I learned Japanese Buddhist, Dr. Mikao Usui, developed Reiki; a universal life energy spiritual practice used since 1922. Reiki is a Japanese treatment in alternative medicine. The Japanese word 'Rei' means "natural Spirit, Holy Gift." 'Ki' is defined as "energy, or vital feeling." Even though we were taught Reiki is a Japanese healing Universal Life Force, it's not affiliated with any Christian or Buddhist faith teaching. The healing art uses symbols from the ancient cultures of India and Tibet which makes it different from other healing energy's modalities. Grounding before, and afterwards, is an important part of this practice. Many practitioners and clients drink a glass of water, hug a tree outside, walk on the grass or sand and let go of the other person's energy by releasing it back to them.

As I lay on the massage table with my clothes on and no shoes, the participants put the palms of their hands on me after asking permission to touch me in pure love. There was soft lighting and low instrumental music playing in the background. The intention was set to balance energy. As I noticed, and became involved, participants' minds were engrossed in a meditative state. While being administered to in this relaxed, calm atmosphere, I could feel a sense of healing touch of heat going throughout my body. I gave myself permission to receive the healing within for restored balance and harmony. The Reiki master took crystals of blue tourmaline and placed them on my Chakra's where she sensed I had an imbalance. Thus, she took out her two-pronged U-shaped tuning fork. Tuning Forks were used on top of crystals to send a vibration of healing into the Chakra areas of my physical body.

     To my amazement, I could feel the harmony that resonated within the frequency of my blocked Chakras. The frequency was felt in my soul and my brain. These areas were blocked, and I was not receiving all the Divine energy flowing from the Infinite Spirit. The Divine energy centers both leave and enter the body. There is so much unknown wisdom from the *Infinite Spirit* for us to understand and one day we will know it all. If one becomes aware of The Twelve Powers and the Hindu system of Chakras, more knowledge, wisdom, the *Infinite Spirit*'s energy and the mysteries of will materialize.

     One of the blockage areas was my solar plexus (3rd Chakra–yellow.) This is the center of all movement in one's soul. The location where I had an imbalance was near the base of my spine close to the navel; near the stomach is where the solar plexus resides. Drops of lemon or rosemary scents were added, and as a result, my personal energy connected to my ego was drained. One's personal and spiritual power, as well as progress, is managed by this area. The third eye, (6th Chakra – indigo,) is the next concentration area. This is the spiritual medium that gives insights of advancement, enhanced intuition, channel information and a clearer knowledge of who I am and who you are too. It is located between the eyebrows. The scents of jasmine, peppermint, etc. may be applied. This is the site of the Pineal Gland area. Remember, this is a Hindu teaching. Thanks to the *Infinite Spirit* for showing us the various vehicles that are used to increase our spiritual mechanism for Infinite Energy. Regardless of your religious belief system, I hope that your minds are opened to allow in this information presented here to flow and comprehend. I bow my head down right now in a sweet surrender unto the wisdom of the *Infinite Spirit*. At this moment in my life I am now starting to learn the practice of Reiki myself because of this personal experience. What I learned that evening was that I had blockages in my energy centers, which had caused me to become slower in my writing. A more detailed recounting of this event can be found in Chapter 6. The short version, however, is that one my energy centers, the 3rd eye, was blocked because I was overwhelmed in my personal life with my step-father's needs in regard to finding him a nursing home to live in. This blockage was causing me to be unable to receive intuitive insights as quickly as I would have liked. I also learned that my Solar Plexus was off, which was hindering my inner wisdom and not allowing me to enhance my writing.

    When massaging others, I am able to tune into their energy centers and help tune their vibrations to a higher plane. Now, I see how important this healing work is for a person's energy centers and to stay focused on the spiritual path. Therefore, I have started to use Reiki in my massages.

Reflecting Back

When I think about the blockages within my energy pathway, I wonder why. For the last twenty-nine months, I have been taking care of my step-father who suffers from Alzheimer's disease. He thinks I am his cousin. As a child he never bonded with me. The last four months have been very challenging to my soul with the issues surrounding his illness. Working with another family member who resists all things that are presented--such as the idea to sell the home so that he may get and stay on Medicaid for long-term care--is quite challenging. My step-father really has not been the problem.

In another stressful situation, my sister recently transitioned this from stage-four cancer at age 42. She left two little children and a husband. I experienced such joy—joy because her suffering is now over, and, at the same time, sadness because she will not be physically present to raise her small children. Then, I look at my life and realize that it does not compare to this suffering. Therefore, I write everyday, regardless of what I am faced with.

Writing brings me complete joy and so does dancing! Being able to be creative and to write helps me to express my god-self. Once you get into the habit and practice, it becomes quite easy, believe me! In the past 29 months I have written five books, taught all types of workshops, taken care of my step-father, shown up for speaking events, and volunteered at church every other Sunday. I have taken a Unity class every Friday from 6 - 8 a.m. for the last nine months and attended a center of worship. I have dated from time to time, have traveled, worked as a massage therapist daily, bonded with friends, listened to and visited my children, attended Metaphysics school online and received my Doctoral Degree. I have also been working full-time on this book! I am a full-time writer; this is my passion! So, you say you can't write anything?

Why?

If I had tuned within my soul, I would have picked up the imbalance; the blockage from the Reiki session. Then, I could have used my god mind and connected with the Universal Mind. In addition, I was not releasing the all of the negative emotions concerning all the challenges of life experienced for the past twenty-nine months. I love the fact that I was open and receptive and gave myself permission to be attuned last night with Reiki. I give thanks to the Infinite Spirit. Now I can buy my own Tuning Folk and use it on myself and on my massage, Reiki and reflexology clients. There are no regrets in my experience. I will go again this week. I would like to encourage you, dear reader, to seek bodywork like massages, healing touch or Reiki for yourself as you enter into your writing projects.

The Twelve Powers of Man/Woman

Let's look at another place that was attuned in my body in contrast to The Twelve Powers centers while I was in a Reiki session. The Solar Plexus, the seat of discernment, the nerve center in the pit of the stomach, is the Law of Wisdom. The disciple represented from the Holy Bible, is James the son of Zebedee. This power is used to bring judgment, discernment and wisdom within one's soul and mind. Think of this as the wonderful color yellow. When activated, the Solar Plexus balances and vibrates and helps one to learn to adjust emotions; its mission is to carry out the Laws of Wisdom for spiritual growth.

Affirm: This day I will call in non-physical beings to help organize, balance, tune in and adapt to Divine Order within my life, world and affairs. So be it!

"Let all things be done decently and in order."
- 1 Corinthians 14:40; KJV

Imagination, my next imbalance that was attuned, was discovered by Fillmore. As I have said before, this is my favorite power. It is represented by disciple Bartholomew; his name was first called Nathanael in the book of John. He sat under a fig tree and later his presence became seen by others. This stands for the fact that things start within the mind then are seen on the outside. Your book starts within the mind and then becomes a physical form! This location, imagination or third eye, is used by people and mediums, (a person who can communicate with the living, as well as the dead) seers (a person who has supernatural abilities to see beyond physical sight) creative or visual artists, musicians and more. There are many people who are able to see things beyond sight, sense, impressions, taste, feel, smell and sound. These gifts have to be developed and practiced. The Imagination link is clearly between the eyes. The color associated with it is light blue. Fillmore understood and taught that a set of tissue went to the back of the brain and reached the picture making function of the optic nerve. Pictures can be from within and without using the power of imagination. Negative thoughts, as well as positive ones will be manifested.

     Affirmation: I now allow shape, forms, tone and colors to shape my mind for an image. So it is!

> "And all of us, with unveiled faces, seeing the glory of the Lord as though reflected in a mirror, are being transformed in the same image from one degree of glory to another; for this comes from the Lord, the Spirit."
> - 2 Corinthians. 3:18; KJV

     September 10; I extend an invitation to the Infinite Spirit, Holy angels and other non-physical beings are now called in for Divine assistance for this writing. The unseen non-physical beings are always present. When we acknowledge their presence and desire their assistance, we perceive more insights. Furthermore, more is added unto us by asking and expecting!

     My orange attraction candle is lit to attract, to me, all my good for writing this day. The content that has been written to you now has been whirling in my head for three days. I can now share with you how to create your desire, supply and demand, if you believe. What do you believe about your writing and the project of funding? The overall theme for this will encompass a question one of my students asked me this past weekend, "How do I fund my book projects?" My answer was, "Basically, I used the 'Law of Attraction and faith' that I will receive my good." It is my personal belief that I am called to write to you; therefore, all my needs are supplied upon the demands. Nonetheless, I see the money floating into my hands, into my bank account and me paying my investments; not debts.

What is the Law of Attraction?
I am going to make it really simple for you to understand. Moreover, whatever you think about, you bring about. That is, for your good or not so good. For example, I am starting a new book project: this one! There are two sets of stages that I will discuss: supply and demand and desire and expectation. One can, and will, attract their good to them by using a mental attitude of supply and demand. As a consequence, when I start my book projects, I must see (the mind's eye) all the invisible supply (people, money, resources, etc.) required to accomplish all that is needed. Also, when supply is needed, I must connect myself with the desires I truly require. If my focus changes, the supply is lost. I miss the mark. However, if I turn another page and focus on the supply in a positive manner, I reach my good and the desire, demand or supply is given. The stipulation for receiving my supply is to learn how to expect fully. There is no time for wanting something and being lazy on the use of the process. Then, it becomes a waste of energy and my important time. However, I must stay focused, steadfast and believe it is all going to show up behind my expectations. Well-intentions are great, but what you put your attention to; you will get. One must expect their desired supply for their book project. Be careful to expect what you want to create for your book project such as affordable editors, the inspirational words, and monetary value to get your books published. You fill the pages with words and sell your books.
This is what I believe:
- Have a clear intention.
- Have a lucid picture of what is preferred.
- Live in the now of what is happening.

- Use the art of spiritual practice or personal soul journaling, silence, meditation and prayer to focus on what is needed.
  (I do this while washing my dishes, before sleeping and while giving and receiving massage.)
- See good unfolding. Use the gift of imagination.
- Release all anxieties. Trust the Infinite Spirit for all things; don't worry.
- Hold an intentional thought of what I would like for my book project
- Give an affirmative Thanks!

Some things are needed regarding funding and time in order to put this book into motion and your book as well. These are ideas that you would take into account and into prayer to the *Infinite Spirit* as you create your inner dialogue. Allow the *Infinite Spirit* to become your partner:

- Research material or books, text content and a subject to write about
- Time set aside to ponder, meditate, and to write
- Proofers, my personal editors, to format graphics, etc.
- Funding
- Time to expound in my personal soul journal
- Office expenses to run my home writing office
- A personal assistant to help organize me and my funding
- Self-publishing costs, Postage costs, again funding
- The cost to send out queries for an Agent
- The time to put a marketing and Query Package together for Agents

- Once an Agent is acquired, the funding for changing of the manuscript
- The daily cost of living and expenses Expenses to and from a workshop, speaking engagement, or class
- Rest, Silence, Meditation and an Affirmative Prayer. Time for me!

This is just my list. Your list as a writer may vary!

I know, in due season, that all things will come to pass if I hold steadfast to my inner visions and dreams. I know this because I didn't go ahead before the Lord. Nevertheless, I didn't move faster than the Lord. I believe what Isaiah said,

"...they that wait on the Lord shall renew their strength."
-- Isaiah 40:31; KJV

Chapter 7

Finding My Way to Spiritual Freedom

"The secret of happiness is freedom. The secret of freedom is courage."
-Thucydides Greek Historian 460-404 BC

In my workshop, students have continually asked me, "How did you get started teaching? How did you get a doctoral degree in Metaphysics?" They also question if I have formal education? I answer quickly with a brief overview while teaching them. At the present moment, I am expounding on the questions that were presented by my students. Subsequently, I reflect on my personal soulful journey from 1998 and where I have been. Do you know your past? Do you know where you have been and where you are going? This is why I stress the importance of writing in a personal soul journal.

Writings from My Personal Soul Journal
Unmasking myself, I am reminded of this line from Charles C. Finn, "Pretending is an art that's second nature to me, don't be fooled, for God's sake, don't be fooled." Therefore, as I consider answers, I contemplate this writing to you during this early morning of September 14, 2011, at 2:30 a. m. In silence, my office is prepared by the burning of the white sage and healing incense. I light a white candle to invite the non-physical beings of Saint Teresa who assists me and others. Now, a forest green candle to represent Divine Order is lit to welcome the Holy Infinite Spirit to abide with me this hour. While working with a Shaman-medicine woman in my area of Nashville, Karen Cressman, she likes to think of herself, in addition, as a Spiritual Initiative, I learned of my animal power spirits. They are an intuitive, lone-male

wolf energy and a small female energy essence of a dog. They both bring me a healthy balance in my life, especially concerning compassion. I am single, not married, and live alone. I am alone a lot. As I understand how the lone wolf works alone and as well with the pack, so I can relate myself to this incredible creature. Most off all I set my action to listen telepathically to my inner guidance within my mind as the lone wolf does so very well. Later, the wolf shares with his pack messages, mind-to-Spirit, for the betterment of the community, so I follow this example. My focus in life is to reach out to the community-at-large.

Many, who are practitioners of animal totem power, may keep this precious secret quiet from others. Nevertheless, I share this with you because you are my students and I feel safe and trust your interest to learn. It's such a special "divination" to learn how the particular animal Spirit and energy can be adapted into your own life, world and affairs. Their messages should not be ignored. The Aura energy field that surrounds my body, that I envision, is cleansed in all directions; my body is luminous. I am clear of negative emotions, physically and spiritually. So many spiritual writers and teachers would like us to think they never experience doubts, fears and concerns. I do; I admit it to you. However, as I reunite with my spiritual practice daily connecting with my Infinite *Spirit*, I am transformed daily. My body, mind, Spirit, world, life and writing affairs are protected by infused white rays of light beaming from my crown to my feet. My writing intentions are set to express a heartfelt gratitude to deliberate my humble beginnings of this spiritual path I have embarked unto. It is my prayer that you receive this information with understanding. At this time, I give an affirmative thanks. So be it.

Beneath it All

The history leading up to my metaphysical, spiritual growth starts here. The emotional abuse I suffered during the twenty-one year dying marriage ended in 1998. One year after my divorce, 1999, my mind was plagued, more than ever, with overwhelming doubts and fears. Those were negative emotions. Inner doubts included: "Can I make it on my own even with child support? Who am I without a husband? What is my true Divine purpose? What defines me? Will I ever marry again?" I asked myself, "Why am I alive at this time?" Mulling over the many masks I wore daily, I thought, "I am just a 'mother of six children'; I use to be a wife, a daughter, a sister, a friend and a woman." Last, I thought, "Is this all that's going to be for me forever?"

When I married my ex-husband, from the very beginning of the marriage, he did not want me to work. I am sure that he wanted to be the only provider. He didn't want me outside the home working or using my God-given Infinite Spirit talents. This made me totally dependent on his financial and emotional care. The talk shows that are on TV now, with so much self-help about controlling behaviors, were not present or not so popular. When he didn't want me to work, I didn't defend my rights to be what the *Infinite Spirit* created me to be. But I have learned and I now take full responsibility. Without being aware of the truth, I had started to repress and suppress my inner feelings, my dreams and my creativity.

The principal at my children's school asked me to be the parent-teacher president. I said, "No." However, once I left and drove to the freeway, a voice within my head said, "Go back and say yes!" Even though I heard the voice, I didn't turn around. I headed home to share the news with the children's father. Excited about the offer, I shared with him the request and he said to me, "You don't have time." With an assurance, I stepped boldly into the next room, picked up the phone, called the principal, and said "Yes!" This work was fulfilled and it ended in 1992. In 1993, I created a ten hour week job at the Metro Nashville School Board district with the encouragement of the director of Metro Schools. I worked in that position for four years. Years later, a thought had popped into my head that the Director of Metro Schools was leaving his position and I believed the inspiration. Later that week, I turned the TV on and to my amazement the announcement of his leaving was spoken. After recovering from shock, I called him. It was true. "What's next, Carol?" I thought.

Thoughts are Prayers
     Mary Baker Eddy, founder of Christian Science Church, wrote in the *Science and Health with the Key to the Scriptures* (1875), "Thoughts unspoken are not unknown to the divine mind. Desire is prayer; and no loss can occur from trusting God with our desires, that they may be molded and exalted before they take form in words and deeds." Our thoughts are prayers, too as we read that passage by Eddy. With this in mind I said to Infinite Spirit, "Please give me a job I can do for the rest of my life."
     I knew I needed to get out of my marriage. In 1997, before filing for divorce, I went to massage school. Years ago I was injured in a car wreck. As a result, I injured my lower back Lumbar Spine 5 and had 80% fibromyalgia (muscle pain/autoimmune deficiency.) I sought natural healing such as Healing Touch with visualization, Yoga, massage, reflexology and herbal

remedies. Little did I know that the *Infinite Spirit* was preparing me for my own massage therapy practice! Remember, I had said a private prayer of desiring a job I could do for the rest of my life.

One day, I was at massage therapy getting a reflexology treatment. A flash of inspiration entered my mind that I could do body work massage and reflexology. I came home to share this exciting news with my husband at that time and he said, "How are you going to pay for it?" I spoke back and said, "If God wants me to attend, then a way to pay will be made." My personal beliefs weren't stuck in deficiency and limitations even though I didn't realize the concept at the time. Within my soul, I knew the opposite was a negative emotional belief. I just knew within my soul if the *Infinite Spirit* wanted me in massage school, then so be it! I eventually entered massage therapy school and was advised to take Yoga back care classes for my own related health concerns. This was the beginning of my understanding of holistic care and my spiritual metaphysical journey.

Attending Traditional Church

Growing up and raising a family in the South, we attended traditional churches. I cannot say I believed everything that was being said or taught. I knew no other way; however, I was always sensitive to the promptings and workings of the *Infinite Spirit* ever since childhood. I grew up a free-thinker, although I was taught to repress my thoughts, expressions and actions. Mostly, I sought other religious sects. So, as a married adult, I went to spiritual counseling from bishops or ministers of the churches we attended. I wanted to resolve the marriage conflict and abuse, but over and over again, there was no consolation. One minister told me that my husband was sick and that was all. I received no help or a clear plan for us. Finally, I convinced my ex-husband to seek marriage counseling with me so we could have a third party's input. That's when I learned I was being emotionally abused and that I needed to free myself from the non-working marriage. Within me I needed to come up with a plan of action to go to school first and then get out of the marriage legally. I didn't share my plans with anyone until I filed and I followed that plan: get in school no matter what and then file for the ending of my marriage. Part of my plan was also to become a successful massage therapist and find out more about who I was in this big world.

After the end of our marriage, I changed churches. The children lived with me part time. I volunteered to decorate the platform of the church on Sundays. One day I had a bad migraine, but I showed up to do my duties. Realizing that my head was hurting so bad, I shared with the minster that I needed to go home. He told me that I shouldn't leave and that I needed to stay and worship. I left and never returned again. This was the start of my disconnection with the *Infinite Spirit*. I thought to myself that my heart was hardening toward religion and its many controlling issues. I then ate my way into forty-three pounds of emotional eating. Again, I suppressed my thoughts about God and spiritual matters. Nothing mattered anymore and my fibromyalgia worsened. Negative thoughts came at me despite the fact I tried to stay positive. A friend shared with me that she went to see an old sage for spiritual counseling. I stated, "I am now free to be, and do, and have whatever I desire after this marriage ends."

A Sage's Wisdom

After learning about this Indian Sage, according to my journal entry in 1999, I made an appointment for spiritual wisdom and insights. We talked about the current events of my life. We were not even talking about religion or churches. She told me to read the Science of Mind publication. She went on to say that Oprah Winfrey reads it. I said, "What is that? Science of Mind?" She explained to me about the Religious Science Centers (the Center for Spiritual Living) and relationship. Next, she looked me in the eyes and said, "You should be in a non-traditional church or you will be sorry." I asked, "Where?" Her suggestions were Unity or Religious Science churches. I was open to this empowering message to my soul. I didn't understand why she said, "I would be sorry." For many years, I questioned that statement. Sunday was coming up and I went to the Religious Science church for my first visit. Being unfamiliar with the terms spoken, I didn't hear anything about Jesus. For many years, as I said, I attended traditional churches. I thought their teachings through Jesus or the Holy Bible were the only truths in Christian Faith. To go to church and not hear the name Jesus was a little different and shocking for me. I was starting to work as a massage therapist in Memphis, Tennessee while I still lived in Nashville. I lived one week in Memphis and another week in Nashville for nine months.

Attending Unity Church

Again, not knowing what the core belief of the Unity movement was, I finally heard the name of Jesus mentioned a few times. After those experiences, I heard the words I needed to hear: Jesus and the Holy Bible. Every now and then, for one year, I would attend the Wednesday night classes at Unity. The messages taught from the books of the co-founders, Charles and Myrtle

Fillmore, resonated within my spiritual side. It was almost like I knew the teachings and they were true for me. It was time for me to move half my time to Memphis. There, in Memphis I joined the Unity Church. The message was the same from the same books. It's now 2005. I am still not clear on "Who I am and what my purpose is." It's time now to focus on me and take my life back. I said, "I am going back to Nashville full time."

Moving Back to Nashville Full Time

The move back from Memphis to Nashville in 2005 was to reclaim my body, mind, and Spirit. I was forty-three pounds overweight. Consciously going through the illness of fibromyalgia and being overweight, I knew the test was on. After joining the gym, a change to wholesome foods, and working slowly to retrain my muscles and mind, I was on my way to developing my spiritual practice. Six months later, I turned on the TV and there had been a model search for women over forty. I remembered right then and there my dreams to model, create, and write books! The contest and model search was put on by More Magazine in New York City. I called them to see when the next contest was. It was one year away. My purpose was shining at that time through my dark, confused soul. Finally, I had clear directions. Creativity was given back to my soul. One year later and 30 pounds lighter, I entered modeling school. Nonetheless, my intentions were to go to New York and be a finalist in the model search. Remember, I moved back to Nashville. Now, I don't attend anyone's church anymore. I am following my gut and my intuition. Now, this was a time of listening to that very small voice within my soul and following those directions. I went nowhere for one year.

Following modeling school one year later in 2006, friends urged me to write my challenges, successes and strengths of the last two years. I didn't want to, but I did, and a book just really came through my soul from my mind to my finger tips. Subsequently, I started going back to the Unity church. I wrote about my wants to create and model as a child. At church that same day, this message was delivered from the church platform by the minister, "It's never too late to live your destiny." That same day in Los Angeles, California, a friend called to tell me about the talk of Dr. Michael Beckwith; the same message within the same day. I asked, "What is going on with me?" to myself. A New Thought minister of mine told me we all are one mind. I didn't understand what she meant then. Keep in mind my goals were to go to New York and model not to comprehend a New Thought message. As of this time, I now understand that there is only one Mind and that is the Mind of the *Infinite Spirit* active in our lives. It is also my deepest understanding that if one person is in California and another is in Atlanta, they can have the same thought at the same time, even if the time zone is not the same. As we are all of one mind, the mind of the *Infinite Spirit*, God or the Universal Mind, this can happen. Therefore, we can have the same thoughts if we are tuned to the higher vibrations of the universe!

My Second Book

In Due Season: Destiny's Calling Your Soul" (2007) is my second book. The title speaks the message of my journey to model at age fifty-one, to live and to create my dreams. However, I wrote about my spiritual and personal transformation as a guidebook. When writing that book, I could feel and perceive a sense of urgency to finish it. The writing task was finished. Within five months, the story lines were done. During that period of February 2007, I didn't get a call from New York for the model search. At that juncture, I was teaching modeling. The agency where I worked had a subcontract with Elite in Atlanta. I asked the owner to submit me and she did. Three weeks later, I was going to interview for Elite and three weeks after that, I moved outside Atlanta.

New Dimensions

This new dimension took me to live in a rural area of Atlanta. It was strange to me being around eighty miles from the city. However, I said, "Yes." I surrendered to the process of my new relocation. My thoughts were, "I came to model", but I started to feel nudges and hunches that I was sent there to write a book. Daily, I went to the tiny county library to search for inspiration and New Thought books. I would order the books that I needed and it took them at least four weeks to make it into the Library system. While living there, I attended a Unity Church thirty miles away. While living in that rural setting, I started to write *Poise for the Runway of Your Life* (2009). My third book was finished in Nashville; the time period took eighteen months. Don't forget while reading this chapter, the question was asked, "How did you get started in Metaphysics?" So many students wanted to know "Just what is Metaphysics?"

Learning Metaphysics

Encarta online Dictionary defines Metaphysics as: The branch of philosophy concerned with the study of the nature of being and beings, existence, beyond, time, and space, and causality; transcend (2011). Even at times they ask me about what metaphysics is. I have to stop and ponder a clear simple answer; this is my duty. Often I say when I was a small child, I understood and knew things beyond the reality of my own mind and soul that transcend time and space. I sense those same feelings as well, beyond my human knowledge.

    When I started my individual studies in 2007 after moving to Georgia, I didn't know what the philosophy of metaphysics was. If you had told me before then that I could tap into the *Infinite Spirit* and create my desired destiny, I would ask, how? All along while growing up and turning into an adult, I have used these simple principles to create what I desired in my heart. While living in that remote area, I read my books, pondered, meditated and was in the silence a lot. I met Saint Teresa of Avila, Saint John of the Cross, Charles and Myrtle Fillmore, Ernest Holmes, and I learned much more about Mother Teresa and many others. Inside that silent place, it became a time for me to learn more about my soul and my purposes in this lifetime. I started teaching a workshop, "Create Your Destiny." As you know, I made preparations to write the third book. In 2009, I moved back to Nashville to begin my life again and to finish the book, "Poise for the Runway of Your Life." The book became a reality in 2009. Then, I took a period of rest from literary work. I started another book *What's Cooking in Your Soul?* (2010.) I dated for a few months and later, once the relationship was over, he mentioned that I should go to the metaphysics school that he was attending. I did the research and enrolled the next day. It was a two-year course online, the University of Metaphysics International School in Sedona, Arizona. One who studies this philosophy, an awakening age-old concept of the mind, learns within things known from the past and unknown truths. They are call metaphysicians. Their purpose in this life is to understand their inner mind and share the knowledge with others. This is simply a way of life; a better way to live this Earthly journey.

In November 2010, I started my metaphysics journey to get a degree, help counsel and write to others. I was able to finish the degree program by March 2011. No, I do not have formal education; I have life education, but I went to the University Seminary of Metaphysics in Sedona, International Metaphysical Ministry and received a Ph.D. First, I finished the first part and lessons in which I became an Ordained Metaphysical Minister and Practitioner and was presented my Bachelor of Metaphysics. Next, I did the requirements for the Masters of Metaphysics after passing the lessons and a 6,000 word thesis. The last requirement was a 10,000 word Doctoral Dissertation. I passed! My dissertation was on my favorite topic, Mystical Research, which I began preparing way back in 2007 in that rural area of complete silence in Georgia! So, this school began my Metaphysics spiritual journey as Dr. Carol S. Batey. Now, I am studying privately the Unity teachings to become a Licensed Teacher.

The ancient practice of Metaphysics existed back many years; some say as way of the East then the West embraced the philosophy/psychology. Within the United States, its humble beginnings started with the Theosophy Movement of Madame Blavatsky. Then, later, Mary Baker Eddy who was deeply influenced by hypnotist Parkus Quimby and more Truth Teachers came afterwards. There are Christian Eastern Metaphysics teachings that were taught by Charles and Myrtle Fillmore who founded the Unity movement. Ernest Holmes, who started the Religious Science (CSL) teachings whose focus was also an Eastern base without a Christian influence, began to attract those who didn't have a Christian background. These, dear, are only a few that I name. I know and understand why the old sage shared with me that I needed to find a non-traditional church. I did not know that I was going to write spiritual and personal transformational books at that time. Yet, that's what I write about to my readership! Was that fate or destiny for me? I have embraced these teaching as a way of life; not a religious walk just on Sunday. I extend to you the invitation to do some inner searching, as well to see what you can adapt into your daily spiritual practices.

    Many New Thought classic books are free to download. Do a search on your personal computer. All of Charles Fillmore's, and his wife's, classic books are free to read online for your spiritual expansion and personal transformation. I am able to write to you with a Metaphysics background because I listened to this age old Sage and my inner guidance! Who are you willing to listen to and follow? Whose promptings for your life will you heed, that may influence your writings? You never know what's ahead, but one must be in tune, open and receptive to the Infinite Spirit's call.

    You, dear writer, are the master of your life, world and affairs; give yourself unto it! Today, October 9, 2011, a little black bird flew into my screen widow into my home. As the little bird flew up and around, he flew toward the lighted area. Once a bird enters your home, they only fly where they see light. Even so, they may fly to a window because of the light they perceive only to hit the glass window and bounce back. The bird looks again for the light to point their way out of my home. The little bird flew into my kitchen window as he/she followed the light. But the bird flew into a fly sticky trap hanging from the ceiling. He/she was trapped. The bird screamed for assistance and to let someone know it was hurt. Feathers were all over that trap. I came into the kitchen he/she was hanging on. I took the broom handle and steer it away, then he/she could not fly for awhile. Next, the little bird started to crawl. I asked, *"Infinite Spirit,* what was this bird totem message to me this day?" I didn't want to miss it. It came to my mind that we also fly high often as humans. Are we aware of where we are headed even though we too, fly toward the light of God, the *Infinite Spirit*? This light shows us the way and often we close our natural eyes and fall into too many traps. Then, we become stuck just like our little bird friend this day. If our inner and outer eyes are constantly headed toward the light of the *Infinite Spirit*, how can we fall into the many traps we fall into? To help my bird friend out, I closed all the doors so that he would not head to the darkness. Birds don't like to fly in darkness; they look towards, and fly to, the light. What message do you receive? Ponder on that thought. There are many; this is only one. Dear writer, when you too are flying high in your world of affairs look toward the light of the *Infinite Spirit*. Once you enter a dark area and you will shut the doors to your outer mind and head only to the light!

> "The master gives himself up to whatever the moment brings."
> - Lao Tse (604 BC- Zhou Dynasty)

Chapter 8

Research is a Must

"The writer is an explorer. Every step is an advance into a new land."
-Ralph Waldo Emerson (1803-1882)

Today, September 15, 2011, I write this to you this afternoon. I will get up early and finish around 2 a.m. My intentions are set to answer the students' and media interviewers' questions that are often asked of me. This afternoon, the editor from Southern Writers Magazine interviewed me to be a feature writer for their July and August 2012 publication. A few of her questions are integrated within this chapter. Also, the editor sent a list of questions that I will provide answers for at the end of this chapter.

Every book or book project begins with a thought that has manifested itself into an idea. This, dear writer, is how story ideas are formulated for literary projects. From the questions asked, a story or book can be pulled together from accurate research. The questions posed are, "How much research do you do for a book?" and "What sacrifices have you made to become a writer?" Thus, both the students and the editor would like me to answer those questions.

Consequently, I am speaking to the writer in you. Research! Research! Research is the first thing a writer must do! Before starting any writing project check to see if the title and concept for a book has already been used. Please pray to the *Infinite Spirit* for directions for this information to be given unto you. Time put into probing and monetary sacrifices spent are a must. You must understand your topic you are writing about deeply so you can work on your plan; execute the messages thoroughly. You have to know how what is selling on the book markets compares to what you thinking of writing. What is the other author's background information and who published and edited their book project? How many pages do the other books have and what is the selling price needed for the book project?

Another importance is setting your intention as an author as to your writing and creating your personal brand. For me, my writing brand is to inspire a personal and spiritual transformation in my readership. As a result, I must seek controversial issues, as well as positive research on my topic. It is imperative to seek both insights to have strong story lines. Therefore, one must have an open mind in order to develop their story ideas. I have to be a critical thinker, a skeptic and have the frame of mind of a reader as well. I can't say this enough to you, dear writer. Research and do more; never stop. You will know within your soul when to begin and end your book project. Often, I feel and sense that my non-physical assistants are not present with me anymore. It's almost like a void occurs. Then, I stop. In order to live and to create my dreams as a full-time author, I've been willing to let go of people, places and things that no longer serve my highest good. For me to get up and write in the early morning before the sun rises, I must go to bed early around 7 p.m. Money that I would have spent going out to dinner, movies or a night on the town goes to virtual assistants. I normally don't date when I am working on a writing project. However, when I am about done, a man usually shows up.

This is what happens to me, it's not set in stone for other writers. Clothes, shoes and personal items bought are the bare minimum until I am finished. My social life is really none when I am writing. Most of my time is solitary; about 90 percent, except for my clients who come to receive body massages or consolation about a spiritual or personal matter. Most of my social life is comprised of going from church to attending my gym classes, thank God. I live alone so I can write at any time. Right now, it is 2 p. m. The only distraction I have at this time is my phone. A large portion of my money goes for everything needed to fund my book. It takes about 1/3 of my living money.

> "Now what I want is facts. Facts alone are wanted in life."
>
> --Charles Dickens (1812-1870)

The Beginning of My Writing Process

     My first process is to do the research to see if the title and information I would like to present is all ready on the literary market. This research should be anyone's first step. You don't want to double what is already out on the market. Then, I need to see how I can prepare something differently in my book that's not currently on the market. I look on Amazon.com, Google books and the public library to see what is published already. I want to also see the impact of the books that are already on the market and who the authors are, as well as examine the author's role for influencing their readership.

     Ideas float into my head and I whirl them around for a few days. I welcome the intuitive vibe from the non-seen beings and give an affirmative thanks. Then, I receive more, and more, an abundance of information given unto my channel to my soul. The messages are given unto my soul by the *Infinite Spirit,* non-physical angels, Spirit teachers, animals or guides. I tell you again, dear one, the books created by you and I are created from the ethers first. The spiritual beings on the other side want us humans to have the book project; therefore, we are used as a channel for good. Each one of the non-physical Celestial beings gives me different messages to my soul. The messages from them come to my soul first. However, it's up to me to be an open channel; a vessel for thoughts of inspiration to float unto me. Then, as I apply my spiritual practice, I remain attuned to the nudging and promptings. When I receive spiritual inspiration, then my writing process starts. One must recognize the beginning of their writings. Often, I receive key words from other materials such as professional journals, written or professional databases, clips, speeches, handouts, press releases, archives of programs or libraries, TV, radio, Internet programs, ministers speaking at my center, hooks from a song, words from another print publication or a person, place or thing, etc.

My second process for writing a book is the verification of research. The most important step is to check all databases and media publications. Check where the evidence comes from. Everything presented on the Internet is not always correct; therefore, make sure other places are checked for accuracy. Cite where the research material that's accumulated is referenced and document this information within your writing. Also, learn to be an observational learner. You can learn many lessons by watching other people and animals. Observe what is happening where you are or if you are doing a live interview, look at the details of events. This is what professional journalists often do. Their personal opinion is left out of the equation for their reports. That is, unless they are writing opinions and editorials, they should present both sides of a story and keep their egos out of it. If you are doing a live interview, don't manipulate the person you are interviewing. Don't change their meaning in what they are sharing with you. Many folks being interviewed live will be reluctant for others to know their names. Be very clear when asking for information or insights. Don't be too broad; be specific, on target. When interviewing, make sure there is no room for their internal alarm to be set off, for them to become defensive. Learn the simple art of listening with your inner ears to hear what they are conveying. Allow the people you are interviewing to make a closing statement and give thanks to them for sharing. Make sure you get their contact information right so that you will have it for contacting them at a later date in case you have to call or email them again.

    From researching, I discover what's already on the market concerning the topic and title I want to create. A market assessment must be done on more than one book. After those concerns are addressed, I will know how to present my results differently from any others on the same or similar topics. I thank God for the Internet; Internet articles and the websites Googlebooks.com, New Thought books online, Amazon.com and many more which make research so easy. Also useful are public libraries, churches, magazine articles, personal interviews, journals, academic statistics that can prove your theory or statistics, documents, school libraries and brick and mortar bookstores (if any are left). There are even church bookstores which are no longer selling physical books. The church bookstores are selling directly from Amazon.com or Barnesandnoble.com with no one actually working in a physical bookstore. Times have really changed.

This investigative book method is on track, it's time to get moving. If a writer's source is the Internet, one would have to see who put the site together and verify if the sources and facts are true. Also, if a writer uses any research, they should cite their findings within their book. It's a pleasure going to the public library. I ask where the books are that I want to investigate. As I walk the aisle looking for books to inspire me, I get chill-bumps; I relate this message to the Infinite Spirit. As I start my exploration, I trust that I am led to the right information with my guides' help. So often I would bring books home only to be awakened to find that I was led by a non-physical guide to the information that I needed.

Keep good notes; file them in folder until the book is done. Don't ever throw away one thing; file it away for future use. Examine your notes over and over in case you missed something that needs to be added to your book project or artistic endeavor. Don't rely on your personal computer alone. Use a flash drive ('jump drive') as well. While starting this book investigation, please keep good notes to refer back to. This inquiry process of the book or artistic project is so important; don't take it lightly and overlook this part. You will need to know this information for yourself before writing a book or starting a creative project. If a live interview was done, record it on an MP3 or some type of recording device to refer back to later. Don't forget to date the recording or your writings so that you are up to date when you did your study. Put in the time for exploration and expenses; it will be worth it.

Focusing on the Process

As you, the writer, focus on your book theme, here are a few things to keep in mind while researching:

- Know your readership; i.e.: age, demographic, diverse background and community.
- Create a brand that speaks to your book. My brand is who I am; Spiritual and Personal Transformation.
- Understand the reader's needs and desires and how you can help them. Answer their questions.
- Know what your book idea concept is about. Keep your book idea in the forefront of your mind. Remember that research will protect your reputation against critics and build your creditability. If you can, be sure to put the information found in your own voice and perspective.
- Know who you need to interview. Know organizations, church or social groups, persons of interest, etc. What's needed for your subject matter and time frame? Where do you go to get your materials? Why are you seeking the information?
- Once you get the amazing essential research for the book material, it's time to write.
- Keep your senses and awareness open to the promptings of the *Infinite Spirit* guiding your feet. When you get stuck, and you will, ask, seek and knock on your soul for assistance from the non-physical guides and teachers. The *Infinite Spirit* is forever present within your soul; however, there are many non-physical guides and teachers signed up to assist our project, as well as our very own

personal angel and the host of angels. The key is to ask, seek and knock as stated in the Holy Bible in Matthew 7:7. Believe when you seek help and you will get everything added unto you! Then, give thanks and move forward.

In the Silence

In the silence of my soul is my perfect time to contemplate and wonder about which direction to explore for creating. Contemplation and wonder are answered by delving into what I want to create. This has been done by hiking in the silence, working out at the gym, turning my phone and personal computer off, driving my car or being quiet in my home for at least one hour. Another sure way is asking and thanking the Infinite Spirit for assistance on helping me to find the information needed, then believing that it will happen. This method, I say again, my spiritual practice, awakens my intuition and heightens my inner focus. Try it for yourself. Trust your inner vibrations. My Guardian angel, a strong male-like energy with tough shoulders, speaks to my mind; telepathically to my soul. My hands are guided to the right publication or phone call to gain knowledge needed for my book research. This particular angel gives me the support and strength needed when I sense I am lost in my writing or there is a blockage (in my personal world, too.) Many times people have given me aide verbally, written in a book, musically, artistically, etc. When I wrote *Poise for the Runway of Your Life*, most of the quotes and inserts in the book were from friends and other materials that were dropped at my feet. Of course my angels, teachers and guides helped along with the *Infinite Spirit*! If you read the book, all the quotes are aligned with the entire subject matter. One day, my funds were low and my friend shared with me how I could go to Googlebooks.com and read a portion of the introduction and some chapters for free. Guess what? My books are there too; not the complete book! Stay open and receptive to insights and look for things that are unexpected.

Just as I get an impression, a clear direction for the writing path, I feel light, as if I am able to fly. The energy I feel is almost like a fairy; it's my female Guardian angel who supplies me in all my creative endeavors. She feels like the "Tinkerbelle" energy. I also feel light, carefree and fun! She helps me to paint, speak, write, cook and to do anything creative. I give thanks to her energy to me and her assistances. When I feel this vibratory of light-fairy energy, I know I am in the right starting place. This fairy-like emotion is felt when I am writing to my readers as well. Sensations come upon me like a flying energy. Have you ever felt or sensed the light-fairy type energy? Do you understand that we all have Guardian angels, as well non-physical beings to assist us on this Earthly path? They help us along our entire Earthly journey. Some guides and teachers will come and go as we work on different book projects, depending upon the subject manner. Our non-physical beings agreed to be with us all our lives. Thanks Infinite Spirit for sending them to Earth too. We are not alone. I leave you the words from songwriter Jack Fowler to ponder (*In the Silence*, www.jackfowler.info).

In the silence there is peace. In the silence there is unspoken joy. In the silence there's relief from a world of chaos and noise. So I wait for these precious moments. When I hear all that could never been said. Right here in the Holy Silence. I find God, I find myself.

Make Use of Everything

    The *Infinite Spirit* will speak to your soul while you are in preparation for your writing project. Pay close attention. At one time in my life, I thought I never heard the still, small voice within me. I thought everyone around me did. However, I discounted my promptings because the promptings from the *Infinite Spirit* didn't come like everything else. My dear, know how the *Infinite Spirit* speaks unto your soul. Pay close attention while at the library, while researching your project on the web, talking to a friend about your subject matter or wherever you may be. Please pay attention to chill bumps up and down the spine. Watch for falling books or someone who may come to you with an answer. Yet, be ever so watchful; let your soul be open, your mind receptive, and be mindful of the various workings of the Spirit. The *Infinite Spirit* will answer your prayers concerning your book research. It is one of my fondest pleasures to read at 1 a.m. on a topic of interest. You see, no phone calls are coming in, no noise; just me and my guides leading me to the right page. There are no distractions! You know why the help comes? It comes because I seek their help. I believe in their guidance and teaching for my soul. What do you believe? It's all magical for me because I believe it will be so and so it is.

    Here's the list of other question asked by the *Southern Magazine* editor. I am going to answer these questions for you here.

1. When did I start writing? What were my first efforts?

    My first writing projects started with my first book *Parents Are Lifesavers* in 1996. I was called on the phone by the acquisition editor to create and develop the book for teachers. At that time, I had no idea that I had so many non-physical beings assisting me in that project.

2. Who are my favorite authors and how have they influenced me?

The author I admire the most is Susan Taylor. She wrote articles in *Essence* magazine and, in turn, the articles were turned into a book. I did the same in *Poise for the Runway* (2009). Following that example it took me 18 months for that book to come to life. The articles became part of my website every month. Then I took half of the article and used it on my blog.

3. Have I had any formal training or writing education?
None whatsoever, actually. I was told when I took a writing test for a class in college that I would never be able to write a book. The next year my first book came out. I have my own academic limitations. However, when I need assistance I draw the right people to me who have the skills to assist me. I know that writing books is my life-path and I step into that call daily.

4. At what point(s) in my career did I feel like I had gone from amateur to pro?

Now that I am working with a Literary Agent, I am learning so much. I am still a new writer. While the agent has encouraged me and suggested revisions for this book, I know this is a part of the process. I remain a student of life and my literary mission is to write my life-lessons.

5. Have I had help along the way? Any mentors?

Yes, the *Infinite Spirit* and the non-physical beings. A lot of my dear friends have served as mentors to me.

6. What's the best writing advice I have received?

    Write in your own voice and from your own perception. Another piece of advice has been that the reader wants to know what is in the chapters that they can relate to.

7. What's the worst?

    Don't write about myself. I had too many "I's" in my stories. I quickly learned that I knew more about me than anything else! So I wrote my life-lessons to my readers.

8. How do you find the time to write?

    Writing is important to me and I am answering the call to bring forth information to this world. I set the time aside daily, regardless of what my other task are.

9. What sacrifices have I made in order to become a writer?

    I have no social life when I am putting my book projects together. I become a hermit until it's over. The sacrifices to me aren't a negative thing; it's just that I put things in my life in a perspective that's important to me.

10. Where did I get book concepts and ideas from?

    From conversations with others, church sermons, needs of people, blogs I read, books, telecasts, networking events, events I have attended, my life lessons; this book, from the classes I teach, music, art, podcasts and my children and family.

11. What were the key ideas that people are seeking?

I want to give my readers answers to their questions they were seeking about how to find their inner Spirit and voice to write books and the process behind publishing them. Most of all I want the students who attend my class to know they can tap into the *Infinite Spirit* to write their books.

12. What steps are involved in book research?

First, I have to decide on how I want to present the material. Then, I find a different way to present my message that's not the same way in another book. The rest is in this chapter. What I want my book to do is to stand out from another one. I create my niche, something that not present in the comparative books that I research. This is the mission that is most important in my mind.

13. Did I choose my genre or did it choose me?

I answered the call to write about Spiritual Empowerment. It chose me. It's my brand, Spiritual and Personal transformation. This mission to help others to unlock their potential to write books chose me, too.

14. What is the best way of marketing my books?
The Internet has made marketing so easy. It basically just takes time set aside to get it done. The time is about three hours a day throughout the day. I still do personal phone calls and send book information by regular email. I love making

eye-to-eye contact with the people I communicate with. I let all my friends on social media know that my books available for purchase.

15. How am I building up my network of readers?

    I build my network through my classes, email listings, art galleries, bookstores, speaking engagements and on social media. My personal clients also buy my books.

16. Am I on social media outlets?

    Yes, I am. I can't sell myself and my books without this medium. I love being able to connect with people and build relationships with those around the world for just the use of my time.

17. What advice would I like to give another aspiring author?

    Believe in your writings, in the call itself to deliver a message to this world. Trust yourself and write, write, write daily. Practice makes perfect.

"I know no thing in the world that has a much power as a word. Sometimes I write one and I look at it until it begins to shine."

- Emily Dickinson (1830- 1886)

Chapter 9

Marketing and Promotions with an Omnipresent Source

"God is the omnipresent source, supply, and support of all creation, and the angels help deliver that supply and support to us."
- Jan M. Howard (N.D.)

    The angelic kingdom awaits your call for help on marketing and promotions. Within this call, one must ask for help in regard to getting the project out into the world where it can do the most good. You should not accept defeat or disappointment as your soul, heart and Spirit are open and receptive to such information. The word omnipresent means something that is everywhere, throughout the entire creation simultaneously. The online- Thesaurus gives another word for omnipresent which is all-pervading. We have all we desire as writers once we tap into the omnipresence of the ever–present source of all our needs and supplies!

    Today, I summon help from the spiritual world. I envision my room full of the white light of protection as I appeal to the non-physical beings from which I desire help. I lit a white candle in order to welcome both the *Infinite Spirit* and non-physical teacher, Saint Teresa. I have placed her picture on my desk. In order to cleanse the area, I am burning Frankincense, which helps to clear the atmosphere and stimulate concentration. I know and believe that this process will help call my divine guides to me. I ask the non-physical beings to provide me with the knowledge of marketing and promotions that needs to be transferred to you, my dear readers. Amen.

"For you, O God, know that which we need and want before we have thought of it and better than we can ever image."
- A prayer from the Armenian Church

Is Marketing Difficult?

Many authors would answer "yes" to this question, as this is one area that most authors fear. Therefore they avoid that which they fear, making marketing hard. However, the world of marketing and promotions within publishing has changed dramatically over the years with the advent of the Internet and social media.

In my classes, I often ask how many of my students are on Facebook or other social media outlets. Usually, only a fraction responds in the affirmative. The other participants make excuses as to why they are not utilizing these resources.

Then, I ask whether their names appear within search engine results when queried. For example, when one types "Spiritual and Personal Transformation" in "Nashville," into a search engine (such as Google or Yahoo!), my website and information is one of the first entries on the list. Such results are free advertising that each and every author should be utilizing.

I also ask my students how many have email lists that they use to contact those interested in their writing. If I am lucky, two or three individuals will answer in the affirmative. Such a response makes me shake my head in disbelief. Each of these questions focuses on simple methods by which to promote yourself and your product, yet very few authors are taking advantage of them!

Some of the excuses that I hear from my students are that they do not know how to use these websites and do not have the time to learn. There is a simple solution to this problem, a solution that I utilize: a personal, virtual assistant. A virtual assistant is a person who completes this work for you. For example, I have a virtual assistant who lives in Indiana, while I live in Tennessee. In the 2 ½ years in which I have worked with her, we have never once spoken on the phone. Instead, all of our communications are conducted via email. If you wish to contact her, she can be reached at emily.heinlen@gmail.com or via her website www.emilyheinlen.com. She completes all of my social media invites for me and has linked my Twitter, Facebook and LinkedIn accounts so that everything that is posted to my Twitter account also posts directly to my Facebook and LinkedIn accounts.

    I also use the editing assistance of Evelyn B. Bourne. She also creates blogs and can be reached via email at ebb567@gmail.com.

    Other students refuse to use social media websites because they are afraid that their identities will be stolen. It is not my job as a teacher to convince the student that they have to be on social media. However, it is my job to help them gain a clearer understanding why this media is now the fastest and most powerful tool for marketing nowadays, and it's basically free. As I educate the students as to the importance of having a Facebook page, that you can use it to connect to your fans and to build relationships with them, they understand a little better. However, a few are still in a resisting mode. I tell them that when you create a fan page it covers only the material you want the public or world to understand about your product, services and goods. Then, a few of them let their guard down and trust that this internet marketing may have a good appeal to their fans.

My students also, often, do not have a personal or professional website. Such a website is imperative when attempting to get your name out to the public and publishing houses. There are a number of resources on the Internet where you can build your own websites for free or inexpensively. I, personally, use the following individuals: www.fredrichfinch.com. It is up to you whether you wish to build your own website or hire someone to build it for you. You must enter into the silence and seek the guidance of the *Infinite Spirit* in order to make this choice.

When your book is complete, make sure that your cover draws attention. Often readers will pick up a book simply because of its cover. Do you create these covers yourself or do you have someone else create them for you? There are many avenues by which you can create a cover yourself. If you have artistic abilities, you can create these covers. For example, for the cover of one of my recent books, I utilized one of my paintings. Or you could take a picture with a camera. If you do not feel that you have the artistic abilities to make the cover yourself, you can hire someone to do it. I have hired a photographer to take still pictures of my work.

I have designed this chapter to help you understand that you have all of the help, tools and abilities necessary to market and promote your writing projects. Remember that you need to be specific in your approach in regard to knowing that you want for your marketing and promotions. You need to know how you want your projects marketed and what you are willing to do. If you get confused or are unsure of how to make a decision, call forth answers, directions, guidance and support from the non-physical beings around you. Angels work for the *Infinite Spirit* and send messages directly to our souls. Sometimes the messages may be delivered by a person, at a particular place or through a thing. It is your job to have an open heart so that the information can be channeled into your soul. For instance; when I wrote the second chapter of this book, Let it Be, the inspiration came while I was listening to a singer at my church sing a Beatles song. I actually began writing the chapter in church.

The beings from the angelic kingdom are God's messengers and, as such, they know God's mind and desires. As good stewards of the Earth and all of heaven's creations, they bring us Divine tools and pure ideas. Their heavenly mission is to work with all of the creatures of the Earth and provide humans the information needed to be productive and successful.

There's a Spanish Proverb that states: "He who does not look ahead, remains behind." Aspiring writers must look ahead toward marketing and promoting their writing projects if they wish to succeed. You must start this process before you begin to write. Do not wait until you are done and then begin looking for marketing and promotions methods. By that time, it will be too late. You must be ready to send your message out into the world as soon as it is complete. If you wait too long, your book will never leave your office and you will never be able to reach your audience. You also will not be able to make money. It is important to note that I do not write in order to make money. I write because I am here to serve you, dear one, and fulfill my writing life path, my destiny. If my mission is completed using the right actions and intentions, then money will come my way. However, the greatest payment that I can receive is to know that needs and desires have been met and that I have been able to serve you with my time, talents and abilities.

What is your mission right now for your writing tasks? Are you writing to make money or fulfill your destiny? Take the time to ponder this question and write your answer here. Be truthful and honest as that is the only way that you will succeed in life and become a better, stronger person and writer.

_____
_____
_____
_____
_____
_____
_____
_____
_____
_____
_____
_____
_____
_____
_____

How do you feel now? Are you empowered? Do you feel motivated to help others and write the project in your soul? If so, start asking your non-physical beings for guidance!

So, Your Project is Done. What now?
Is your writing project completed or almost completed? Where are you in the process? Did you conduct research before you started to write? Have you created CDs, MP3s, apps, podcasts, music, books or DVDs that you want the public to know about? Are you able to turn your writing projects into recordings that you can place on

your website and use for marketing or promotions? Are you now wondering what the next stop in the process is? I know that I have pondered these same questions many times. Have you asked the *Infinite Spirit* what to do next for your marketing? In order to know the next step in the process, you must ask for guidance. I have had to do this on a number of occasions. You must also examine your true feelings about starting your own publishing company for books or music. Maybe you have been trying to seek a song pitcher or a book literary agent and nothing has happened. You just may want to start your own publishing company with you as the publisher. Living in Nashville and teaching writing classes, I have many students who have dual roles, as they are both authors and songwriters. So, I offer material on writing for both. Starting your own independent publishing company on the internet gives you the advantage of being in-charge of your published works. Make a publisher come to you by making an internet presence and a world platform. If you start your own publishing company, then you own the rights to everything you create and the funding for the company is your responsibility as well. You can also go to your state's Secretary of State office and create an official corporation.

    How do you feel about self-publishing, digital publishing or on-demand publishing?
When you self-publish, you basically start your own publishing company. You own all the rights and all the profits are yours. In Nashville, there is lightening source, a division of Ingram, where an author can walk in, set up an account and publish for a per book fee and a one time set-up fee. Digital publishing is the new way to break into the publishing industry. You can publish your books for free on Amazon and at Barnes and Noble. You must have

the book ready for review. Then, it will be placed on various sites for purchase. Contracts are there to set up accounts and royalties. Print-on-demand sites are sites where you submit your artistic works and you can order one copy or three hundred. You receive a royalty check from sales that include their website and other outlets, such as Amazon.com.

Do you understand what is needed in order to self-publish? Are you marketing savvy enough to step out on your own with the *Infinite Spirit* as you partner? If not, within this chapter, you will find the encouragement that you will need to move from selling your product out the trunk of your car and to your friends and family to selling to a worldwide audience.

First, marketing is not what it used to be thanks to the Internet. When you begin the marketing process, you should ask Archangel Gabriel for insights into the many ways that you can utilize the Internet to sell and promote your projects. As you read this chapter, you may want to write additional notes in a notebook or journal.

Below, I will discuss several marketing methods that you can use.

An MP3 is a digital audio file. MP3s can be created using many free or purchased software projects. Many authors record their interviews, chapters and web or telephone classes using this format. One way to utilize MP3s as a marketing technique is to offer a free MP3 class if an individual signs up for your newsletter. Or you can provide the MP3 class on your website, for free or a fee, for those who missed the live version of the event. I often offer MP3s of past classes on my website for a small fee. This method is very effective in regard to marketing yourself as a brand.

An app is an application or software that can be downloaded to a phone, computer or other electronic device. These apps can be in the form of a game or informative program. For example, I am considering creating an app called *50 Simple Solutions to Life Transformations*, which will provide easy answers to every day life questions. I would sell this app in app stores and on my website for a one-time price of $4.99. You can do the same and use it as a marketing tool or promotion for your books, services or products. This app could be downloaded to an iPad, phone, personal computer, Kindle or Nook.

While writing this chapter, I realized that many aspiring writers fear marketing their services and products on the Internet. This fear occurs because they lack an understanding of how and why Internet marketing is necessary. As an author who uses the Internet to market and promote my goods and services, I wish I could come to each of my reader's homes and help them on this journey, but I cannot, as the products that you are promoting are yours and yours alone and I am only the catalyst to be used to drive, inspire and direct you onto your writing path. Therefore, in order to inspire you, I am going to introduce you to the Ascending Master Saint Germain.

Who is Saint Germain?
Saint Germain was born in Europe in the late 1600s. He was a gifted and talented man who devoted his life to a service to God. His mission or branding to me is a "spiritual and personal mission for transformation and deep spiritual communion." The deep spiritual communion is developed in a bond with the *Infinite Spirit*. He can offer you, my dear reader, a deeper sense

of writing and marketing growth as well as a higher spiritual consciousness for your life.

Can you envision a violet flame? Do you see it? See that flame burning away all of your inner fears about marketing and promotions. Let all of your excuses burn into smoke. See the smoke being carried up into the ethers of the heavens. As your human ego (self) shrinks, allow the I AM presence of the *Infinite Spirit* to be integrated into your soul. Set your fears and inner doubts aside and allow God to manifest. Let him help you understand your marketing concept. Be peaceful in your heart; see that violet flame going to all parts of your body. See it enter each of the seven chakra's that activate your energy. Let it replace all of the fears, self-doubts and worries that you have about how to get your message out to the public. Put a warm smile on your face that will be recognized inside your soul. Know that you are an expression of the *Infinite Spirit*. Learn to ask the heavenly non-physical beings for help. Let go of your pride and become humble.

"As a child of the universe, Saint Germain states that you can learn whatever you put your mind to. Yes, I often cause a stir in people in charge, but I never give in to doubts and fears. Neither shall you! I have called upon you, have you heard? Then, know that you can call upon me. I will assist you, soul and mind, in your marketing plan for the Internet. Your work is important. Don't ever stop inviting the non-physical beings from participating in your work. Wherever you are, we are there also. I am here for you. Just ask for direction, courage and the ability to understand how to use the Internet. Then, wait calmly and see the color of violet. Simply say that 'I have a desire to serve humankind with my God-gifts and talents' and I will be there" As spoken to Carol by Saint Germain. So it is.

What is Your Brand?

You may say, "Carol, I am a writer. What does the branding of a product or services have to do with me? That is just more work for me to do. I just want to write books, not do the rest." In today's society, you must connect with others and build a personal relationship with your consumers. You need to market your goods and services directly to the individual. Today, you can cut out the middle man who used to go between you and the consumer. By cutting out this middle man, you will have to divide your profit up between less individuals. In addition, by marketing directly to the consumers, you can form lasting business and fan partnerships that can benefit you in the long run.

Keep in mind that I am still old school in that I try to send things out via postal mail and I use my phone to make daily calls. However, I mix these strategies with new, Internet-based strategies. The first thing that you need to do is make sure that your consumers can find you when they search for you in a search engine. In order to be easily found, you must create a brand that is identifiable and directly relatable to you. My brand is Are you Ready for a Spiritual and Personal Transformation? If you search for this phrase in a search engine, one of the top results will be my webpage. A writer or creative person should be able to identify his or her creative brand in 15 seconds or less. Can you? Your brand should reflect your products and services and have a unique name and image related to your products and services. Write your brand here in 15 words or less:

Self-Promotions

Do you believe in yourself and your services? Be honest. Take a few deep breaths and tap into your 3rd Chakra, your Solar Plexus, as you inhale. Hold the breath for 10 counts and imagine the color yellow as you release the breath from your nostrils. Then, answer whether you believe in your writing projects and yourself? Yes or No.

___

Marketing your products or services and self-promotion are intertwined. Have you ever heard of the saying that "you are what you eat"? Well, you are what you write and promote. Your project represents you and who you are. If you have a healthy outlook about yourself, then it will be easier to promote yourself. You have to sell yourself to others before you can attempt to sell your projects. Who are you? How do you feel about yourself? Be honest with your answers.

_____
_____
_____
_____
_____
_____
_____
_____
_____
_____
_____
_____
_____
_____
_____
_____

Pretend that you have been introduced to a writer who has an inspired product, but a negative self-image. Would you purchase a product from this person? What would you say to this person about his or her self-image issues? Write your answer below.

Here is my answer...
Dear writer,
    You have been called to Earth to bring into existence an important literary work. I will ask the Egyptian goddess Isis to intervene on your behalf. I wish for you to have a stronger self-worth. I wish for you to love yourself so that this love shines through to everyone who meets you. When you begin to punish yourself due

to the negative core beliefs that you hold, please call upon Isis and let her help you to become the person you can become. She will lift your spirits and improve your self-esteem. You will feel your soul rise above your low self-esteem and will find your confidence in no time. You must simply open your heart to allow her influence in. Let it flow through you. You are a strong person. Often, we forget who we are. Remember that you are the child of the *Infinite Spirit*. You were made in his image and likeness. Whatever the *Infinite Spirit* has done so can you. Learn how to use the Internet! So it is.

If you are seeking to enhance your skills in regard to marketing and promotions, then I encourage you to read my book *Why Aren't You Writing?* (2011).

Chapter 10

Be True To What You Believe

"Other people's opinion of you does not have to become your reality."
- Les Brown (1945-present)

In the last two years, my students and close friends have posed this question, "How do you write about your personal and family relationships?" Often, they ask this question because of their own experiences with sexual, emotional, mental and physical abuse; family and friendship betrayal; or because they have personal messages that they want to share, brought about by a wonderful or sad childhood or their experiences as an adult. More than a few of these individuals have suffered one or more of these sensitive and indescribable actions. Yet, even though their inner wounds scream out loud, they are unable to share their messages with the world. They want to learn how to rewrite their lives and turn the page so that they can move forward. Are you willing to share your lit candle with the world? Can you do so if it will reveal the deep, dark secrets that you keep hidden behind your many masks? These hidden masks allow us to present the face that we want the world to see. They allow us to tell the world that we are fine, even when things are not as they seem. Telling your truth of who you are and your perspective on what you believe and what you are isn't always easy. However, you can do it: one word and one page at a time. You must believe in your personal truth.

Dear Writer, your message needs to be told to help heal and inspire others. You are here to write books and make this world a better place. Your guides, teachers and the *Infinite Spirit* want your message to come through you.

Being a Vessel of Light

Jesus said in Matthew 5:14 (KJV), "Ye are the light of the world..." You, my dear writer, are a beacon of light that is needed so that you can share your truth for those who have suffered and are still silently suffering the pain that you feel. Your divine message has been given to you to share by the *Infinite Spirit* for purposes of healing. Healing and reconnecting other peoples' inner souls with your message will set them free! When I am writing a message about pain and suffering, the elements of which make me feel vulnerable, I feel strange. I especially feel this way when writing about the emotional pain or sexual abuse inflicted upon me. Therefore, when writing such passages, I need to look deep within myself and discover why I am writing this information to share with others. What is my purpose, my goal? Knowing that information makes the writing easier to handle. I have learned to enter into the holy silence and find my inner awareness so that I can speak the truth of my mind freely.

Another aspect of writing that you must consider is what voice you want your readers to hear. Do you want them to hear a voice of negativity, no hope, despair, anger, heartlessness, envy, fears, resentment and distrust? I don't. I want my readers to sense that I am a victim of my circumstances, only.

Did you know that if you carry around negative thoughts and emotions, it can negatively affect your health? This information is another reason why I choose to write about my past experiences. These negative thoughts and emotions can cause your body to produce diseases, including an impaired immune system, cancer, liver and heart problems and cold sores. These problems occur because these negative thoughts and emotions block the body's energy centers. In order to purge these emotions and not give them additional power over your body, make sure that you try to keep your emotions at bay when recounting a past experience. Make sure that your reasons for writing down an experience are to share how you have overcome the situation and grown from it, not to harm others. Only by letting go of these emotions and thoughts will you be able to rise above the situation or experience.

Many times, my students will come to my classes and then, also, come to me for metaphysical counseling, especially if they have been previously sexually or physically abused. In these sessions, they often ask me how to write about their personal experiences. Once they are able to clearly explain why they want to write about their experiences, they have taken the first step to finding their voice and beginning to heal.

Forgiveness Works

Once you have looked into your heart and discovered why you want to write your message, you must look inward again and reexamine the situation in order to discover the absolute truth about what happened and why. You must make sure that you are stating only the facts and not any opinions or bias that you may hold against the situation. I have found that many of the things that I felt were truths were actually illusions that I had created within my mind. For example, when I realized that I could become a model at 50-years-old, I changed the way that I thought and my belief system about my ex-husband and mother. I had thought that they had sabotage my modeling and creative career, when really, it had just begun. Once I let these misconceptions float away, I was able to let go of my negative thoughts and emotions toward them, which was my old way of thinking.

Another thing that I realized after embracing the New Thought Truth Teachings is that those I allow into my life both teach me and receive teachings from me. In order to write about my past, I had to accept this truth. Once I accepted this information, I could accept that I am the co-creator of my divine destiny. By taking ownership of my destiny, I set myself free and let go of my negative baggage. Once I began letting go, I realized that it was my own thoughts about my mother and ex-husband that were holding me back, not them. Therefore, the key when writing is to be truthful and true to the reality of the situation. That's the only way to clearly present what really happened.

Setting Goals with a Focus

Once I have prepared myself to write, I write down my goal for the particular project that I am working on. What do I want to share with the audience? How do I want to accomplish the end result? In order to answer these questions, I enter into contemplative prayer. It is important to note that there is a big difference between contemplative prayer and meditation. During contemplative prayer, my focus is on what I want my readers to gain from this particular project. I ask for the knowledge to help my readers gain that knowledge. I pull my inner awareness toward my heart and solar plexus in order to gain spiritual wisdom. Here is an example of what I think about during a contemplative prayer: I choose a word to focus on, for example, forgiveness.

Then, I decide who or what I need or desire to forgive. Then, I write an affirmation statement about whom or what I want to forgive. Here's my affirmation: I choose this day and everyday to forgive my mother and ex-husband whom I thought didn't let me become the creative person I wished to be. I use this time for inner growth and acceptance. I usually spend between five and ten minutes on such a prayer. If I do not receive an answer, I keep the prayer close to my heart all day until I know what to do.

In her book, *Book of My Life, Introduction* (2007), my non-physical guide, St. Teresa, shares the three types of contemplative prayer:

- A recollection is when we release into a stillness and let go of all concerns and focus our attention one-way to God. "Contemplative prayer teaches us to be mindful of what we are doing."
- The Prayer of Quiet is simply being still into the holy silence of your soul and making no noise; thinking nothing. Let go of the intellect. Try not to become distracted by the outside world. A quiet serenity will occur often in this moment of a spiritual practice being in the silence.
- The Prayer of Divine Union is a union of the god-self and *Infinite Spirit* as one. Living with a connection to the Divine is a spiritual marriage. I believe that changes happen within us when our souls are united with God. We must utilize our spiritual practices in order to remain in this union with God. As this union grows, you will feel a light grow within your body. When you are united with God, you and God are one.

Do you have a spiritual practice in place yet? I have asked you so many time throughout this book, "Do you have a spiritual practice in place?" If you intend to write with the *Infinite Spirit,* then it is time to share, turn on your light and turn it up.

"You are a Genius, a Prolific Writer. A city that is set on a hill cannot be hidden"
-- Matthew 5:15; KJV

Do not hide your story. What are your intentions for your story?

_____
_____
_____
_____
_____
_____
_____
_____
_____

"Nor do they light a lamp and put it under a basket, but on a lamp stand..."
-- Matthew 5:15; KJV

Why do you want to share your story?

_____
_____
_____
_____

_____
_____

> *"...and it gives light to all who are in the house."*
> *-- Matthew 5:15; KJV*

What results do you want your readership to gain from reading your story? How do you want to share your personal story? For what purpose do you want to share it?

_____
_____
_____
_____
_____
_____
_____
_____

> *"Let your light so shine before men, that they may see your good works and glorify your Father in heaven."*
> *-- Matthew 5:16; KJV*

Tell your truth. Don't seek harm while writing to another person; just bless them. Remember that your light is shining brightly.

Chapter 11

All Things are Spiritual: Destiny's Calling Your Soul

> "We do not create our destiny; we participate in its unfolding. Synchronicity works as a catalyst toward the working out of that destiny."
> - David Richo (N.D.)

Today, September 28, 2011, I write to you at 6 a.m. while I am sick in bed. I brought my laptop to bed with me! Soft music plays and the lights from outside the house light the area in which I am working. I send an invitation out to my non-physical guides and teachers to provide me with the insight and knowledge necessary to write on this delicate topic. Dear writers, do you hear with your inner voice? Is it telling you that destiny is calling your soul, telling you to write books? Do you believe you were preordained to complete a book before you were born onto this Earth? What does fate have to do with your path to write books? Fate is often related to destiny as a fixed decrier of order. If your fate is to write books, then it's predestined. Search your soul for the inner meaning of what destiny or fate means to your book writing career. What does destiny mean to you?

Many authors, ministers, mystics, ancient sages, teachers and inspirational speakers have told us that everything we do is part of a spiritual mission for the *Infinite Spirit*. Everything in our lives is spiritual. For example, every time a coincidence happened in my life over the course of the past year, I called my dear friend, Reverend Alice J. Brown, to share my findings. She would always tell me that everything in life is a spiritual mission. For instance, once I broke off a romantic relationship with a man, but he refused to see that it was over. He continued to show up everywhere I went and texted me daily about his daily and future plans. Regardless of how many times I asked him to leave me alone, he would not heed my pleas. He simply acted as if I had never spoken. Finally, I asked the *Infinite Spirit* to make me understand why I was still running into my ex. When I was still, and in contemplative prayer, I heard a message from the *Infinite Spirit* telling me to write about this issue in a relationship book. The *Infinite Spirit* said, "Carol, you think that you have been stalked, but there are so many more men and women who are stalked by those who wish to do them bodily harm." If I had not constantly run into him, then I would have not realized that there was more to the chapter that needed to be written.

These coincidences, such as receiving this information as I was writing a book on the topic, happened to me daily. I would ask the *Infinite Spirit* if these events were just coincidences or something more. One of the messages that I received when I kept running into my former partner was that I needed to write something on how to let go and move forward after a relationship ends. Even though I was not in any harm or danger from this man, this lesson was the one that the *Infinite Spirit* wanted me to share. At that time, I was writing a book about how to move on after a divorce. Therefore, this experience was one more that I could add to the book to strengthen its message, while, at the same time, allowing me to examine my feelings for this man.

In order to keep track of these coincidences, I keep a soul journal in which I write down events or interactions that I have been involved with throughout the day. I find that reviewing this journal lets me better understand what I have experienced in life and where to go next. I find that every coincidence has a meaning to my life. The same is true for your life.

Carl Jung (1952), the famous Swiss psychiatrist, coined the word synchronicity to mean: "temporally coincidence occurrences of more than one events." He described an acausal event as a "connecting principle." Jung believed that for synchronicity to be true, two or more connecting events needed to be happening at the same time. Such an instance is often called a coincidence. It is also important that these events produce a meaningful experience to at least one of the individuals involved in the event. These coincidences are sometimes also called luck, good fortune and serendipity.

Jung thought that everyone had a spiritual mission and purpose that went beyond owning material goods. Our innate potential is to connect and understand our higher self and the *Infinite Spirit* (also known as the Divine). Have you ever thought about a person and then had them call? On many occasions, I have had a thought enter my mind and, within a few minutes, that thought was manifested into what I was thinking of. An example of this can be found in that one day I was in need of $253. Instead of worrying about the issue, I surrendered my worries and asked the *Infinite Spirit* for help manifesting that amount. Later that day, one of my clients called and asked for a massage. After the massage, he asked if he could prepay for a month's worth of services. His prepayment solved my monetary issue.

Believe in Synchronicities

What do you, my dear writer, believe about synchronicities? Have you ever had two more events occur close to one another that seemed to be unrelated, but reacted in a meaningful way in your life? If so, they were synchronicities. For example, one day, I realized I needed someone to edit my writing project. Later that day, I booked a massage with a client. After talking to the client, I discovered that he was an editor. We exchanged numbers and he began to work for me.

Many cultures believe in synchronicities, including the Native Americans. In their culture, they place a focus on how they accept these actions (synchronicities) as the truth. Native American traditions have taught their people to direct their innate attention to the timing of, and lessons from, hidden messages. In order to direct your attention toward these messages, you must first be aware of what is happening in your life, world affairs and understand that your human psyche is tied to physical manifestations within the world at-large. I believe that I kept running into my former partner because one, or both of us, was not ready to let go of the relationship. It is my belief that the hidden message was being given to him and I was being used as the messenger.

Sometimes you may not understand the importance of an experience until later or, you may receive a message from the *Infinite Spirit* while still experiencing it. For example, one day, while flying home from Charlotte, North Carolina, the plane that I was on was delayed by 45 minutes. As I knew that this would reduce the time that I had to make my transfer flight at the Atlanta airport, I rushed to the connecting gate as soon as I arrived. However, once I arrived, I learned that this plane was also delayed. First, it was delayed by an hour and then two. I asked the *Infinite Spirit* for guidance and he reminded me that I am always on a mission from God, even when it doesn't seem like it. Finally, we were told that the flight would be delayed for four hours.

Instead of decrying the inconvenience, I chose to make the most of the time and seize the day.

The Latin words for seize the day are carpe diem, which mean to gather, crop, pluck, pick or make use of. That day, I decided to strike up conversations with the others waiting for the plane. We talked, shared and complained. I told one man that I wrote books. Then, Randy Owens from the country group Alabama came in to where we were sitting. The people around me were very excited to see him and wanted to get his autograph. As I had been his massage therapist years ago, I went up and reintroduced myself to him. Noticing how tired he was, I offered to massage his shoulders. I spent the rest of the delay massaging his shoulders, as well as the shoulders of others in the airport. Randy even asked for my number so that he could call me later for another massage!

While I was spending time with Randy, the man to whom I had told that I wrote books, told another woman. She just happened to be Alexandria Altman, the well-known author of the Cinderella Chronicles. We were introduced and became engrossed in a conversation about the publishing industry. Then, she offered to introduce me to her publisher. Since then, she and I have spoken on the phone several times. She has asked for my help on how to learn to teach others to write. We are making plans to present a workshop together. In another twist, we learned that we attended the same Metaphysics school 10 years ago at the University of Metaphysics in Sedona. Just think of all the opportunities that I would have missed out on if I had not spent my time interacting with others during the delay.

I started writing this chapter with you, my dear readers, in mind. Yesterday, I went to the gym to see if I could sweat some of the toxins out of my system. I couldn't make it through the hour long work out; I was too sick and weak, so I left. As I was packing to leave, a woman named Jane, who I often saw at the gym, arrived. I told her to take my spot as I was leaving. Later that evening, I received a phone call from Dr. Jane Miller, who said that she was the assistant principal at Saint John's School. Her friend Joyce had suggested that she sign-up for one of my workshops on how to write books. I told her that Joyce had attended my class six weeks earlier. Jane informed me that "This is funny. This is no one but God putting this all together. I picked up your flyer on the topic last night at the gym." I then mused out loud whether she was the lady to whom I gave my spot at the gym the night before. She stated that she was and said that "This is no accident; it is all God."

As we continued to talk, I discovered that she would not be in town during the next workshop. I suggested that I could do a workshop at her school for the parents, staff and community. She liked my idea and asked me to come by the school the next week to talk about it. I agreed and told her that I also provided one-on-one sessions if she was interested. She was!

This story, once again, illustrates how something minor can turn out to be a big influence on your path and journey. You must always be open to listening to the *Infinite Spirit* and hearing his guidance. Ask him for help and then listen closely for the answer. He will provide you with a message.

Do not become complacent in your spiritual practices. If you are unwilling to participate in meditation, prayer and affirmative prayer, then you will not be open to hearing the *Infinite Spirit*'s messages. Make sure that you keep your inner ears open and attuned to his voice. Keep your soul cleansed and fresh in order to welcome the non-physical guides and teachers. Keep your heart open and receptive to the promptings of the *Infinite Spirit's* ways. Be open to seeing your muse, as it will guide you and inspire you. Keep in mind that you are the channel through which the *Infinite Spirit* is talking to your readers and those around you.

Chapter 12

Questions and Answers: The Discovery

"The intellect has little to do on the road to discovery. There comes a leap in consciousness, call it intuition or what you will, and their solution comes to you and you don't know how or why."
- Albert Einstein (1879-1955)

Within this chapter, I will answer the rest of the questions students have presented to me. Most inquiries are presented on the topic of why they can't write their projects.

Students: I cannot finish my book because I make excuses.

Teacher: My first question is how important the book writing project is to them. If the writer is answering the call to write, then they will make the time to finish the project one day at a time. One must see the book project in their mind's eye from beginning to end. Visualization is one of the keys. Use your gift of imagination to produce your project.

"Like so many generals when plans have gone wrong, I could find plenty of excuses, but only one reason- myself."

— William Slim (1891-1970)

Students: Who wants to read my stories in a book?

Teacher: Do you believe you are called by *Infinite Spirit* to write a message of hope and inspiration to this world? Why do you think you have experienced the ups and downs of your life, world and affairs? Because you have a message to deliver, remember you are a prolific writer called by the *Infinite Spirit*. You must believe in your calling; no one can give you that assurance. You must know down in your gut that this is for you to do and move forward.

> "God didn't put me on this Earth to be a loser. I'm a winner."
> —Sparky Anderson (1934-)

Students: What do I have to say?

Teacher: Do you have trust and confidence in your ability to write and communicate with your readership? If you stop forcing things within yourself, it will happen. Believe in yourself and what you are here to accomplish during your Earthly existence. You have a lot to say; ask the non-physical guides and teachers, along with the host of angels, to assist you. You must believe and trust the process. Use your spiritual practice to increase your leverage to write books. Apply faith and trust in the *Infinite Spirit* for wisdom and guidance.

> "With the exercise of self-trust new powers shall appear."
> —Ralph Waldo Emerson (1803-1862)

Students: Why do I sabotage myself?

Teacher: Do you understand, dear one, that when you self-sabotage you set up a roadblock to your success. You create your own destiny or fate! Your thoughts, feelings and actions either enhance your life or hey don't. It depends on your level of emotions. If the emotions are positive, then you are on your way to success. Now, if your emotional sense is on the negative side, then you feel frustrated and may stop your own destiny. Fear of success is usually the main reason for self-sabotaging. Then, for a person who exhibits a low self-esteem, unworthiness and low-confidence, this person is on a destructive path. The power is within you to succeed or not. I know you can, do you? My dear, can you write yourself an affirmation of your worthiness as a writer? For example: "I am a wonderful communicator and talented writer."

"My inner self was a house divided against itself."
–St. Augustine (A.D. 354-430)

Students: My problem is I fear rejection.
Teacher: How many times have the messages of Masters, Sages, Mystics and Leaders, etc. in this world been rejected? Rejection is a part of literary work. One must have a thick skin and truly believe in their literary works. I have received many rejections from readers who hold traditional religious beliefs. As I look for literary agents and publishers, I know that I will be rejected. Everyone is not looking for my book material to shop and purchase. The right alignment vibration must be matched to the writer, literary agent and publisher. Everyone must be on the same page. Then, I also know I must be ready and willing to change whatever is suggested. Can you do that? I am a model. When I don't get a casting once I audition, is it because I am not good enough? Is it because I am too short? No, it is because I don't have the right match for what the director is looking for. After many rejections, I finally I know I will get a 'yes' soon enough. I apply my faith and perseverance. You can too.

> "Words are…the most powerful drug used by mankind."
> --Rudyard Kipling (1865-1936)

Students: I don't understand the book writing process.

Teacher: Everyone's writing process is different from others writers. It's my belief that one should do what feels right for them. You may have a 9-to-5 job, so you will have to create a schedule that works for you. For example, you may be married with no children and your husband doesn't get home until 9 p.m. As a dedicated writer, you may want to write for two hours once you get home and cook dinner. Now, if you are one who works at home and can set your own time, you may want to begin writing very early before you start your day. Once you get in the habit of setting the time aside to write, it becomes very easy for you. Some writers start after their research with an outline from beginning to ending of what they want in their book. On the other hand, there are many who don't create an outline and just start the process of writing after researching. Make a writing business and marketing plan. Start making an author's platform by developing a presence on the internet. Many authors used blogs to communicate with an audience and get feedback. Then, don't forget to make sure you are present on as many social media networks as possible; the new way of marketing and promotions. Do you have a book website even though the book is not finished? What about using YouTube; yes, even before the book is completed? Are you already teaching and speaking on your topic you would like to write about? Begin writing articles on your topic of interest; there are over 1000 sites where you can place free articles. Type free articles on a search engine on your personal computer and seek the topic you want to write about. For instance, I use self-growth.com and my topic of interest is personal development. The most important job for a writer is to write daily, regardless of time, work load and a writer's lack of understanding of the process. Create your own process what works well for you. What time is best for your writing? How long in a day can you devote to your writing craft? How much time daily can you put into researching materials? How much money will be needed to start, and then to finish, the writing project? Assess if you, the writer, may need to go to a quiet place away from the home to write. If, so where could you go? You have the answers within your soul for what is right for you. Most importantly, make a commitment to yourself and the book writing project.

> "It is by sitting down to write every morning that one becomes a writer."
> --Gerald Brenan (1894-1987)

Students: How do I find a literary agent and why?

Teacher: This has been one of my greatest challenges. Anything you desire enough by using the Law of Attraction, can be attained in due season. A writer must exercise faith, use the gift of imagination, have persistence and don't give into 'this just is taking too long' mentality. Most people use the Writers Guide publication (agentquery.comsearch.aspx) to research literary agents. You can find others on the internet just by typing 'literary agent'. Once you locate the list of agents, then, if you are a science fiction writer, type in the topic you fall under. Follow the guidelines. If the site says you can query by email, follow the directions and only email. Often, the site may say query by regular mail, then do as the site directs you. It may also ask you to send a self- addressed stamped envelope (SASE) for corresponding information. Another way of seeking a literary agent is to read books similar to the book you are writing. Read everything within the acknowledgement pages; know who the editor is for that book and the Literary Agent as well. If you know someone who has had a book published by a conventional publisher, they probably had an agent. Ask them if they would recommend the agent to you and for you. Don't lose your faith in the search and make sure you all are a match. In order to reach the conventional publishing gates, a writer should acquire a literary agent. They are the key to the gate keepers. A writer can always self- publish, therefore omitting all the years of rejection from literary agents.

    This summer, I attended a literary conference and I had two literary agents ask me to put a proposal together. I did and I am now working with one of them.

"Writing came easy—it would only get hard when I got better at it."
- Gary Wills (N.D.)

Students: I am a private person; I want to tell my own story. I don't want the world knowing about me.
Teacher: If this is so, maybe you are the one to write this type of project. So you are saying, I don't want the world to know my personal business, but I have a story to share with the world. Make up your mind, dear one. Are you the one to share this personal book work? You, dear writer, could write a fiction book with some truth to the story lines. The places, names and subject story lines can be changed. Once you choose to do this book project,

find your niche and message within the story lines. Everyone I meet has a book or two inside their soul, but the writer has a lot of competition with others. Again, make your book different from another author's book.

> "Uncomfortable truths travel with difficulty."
> - Primo Levi (1919-1987)

Chapter 13

Saint Teresa, One of My Writing Partners

"True mystics simply open their souls to the oncoming wave."
-Henri Bergson (1859-1941)

In closing, you probably have wondered why I know who one of my non-physical writing partners is. This person has also guided my soul, when I felt lost in this world, through her books. Through her books and her life lessons, she has taught me valuable lessons as my teacher. One thing she taught me is that perfection is attainable day by day through a spiritual practice. She is the astonishing mystic Saint Teresa of Avila from the 16th century. The words she has written about her own writing path speak to me. What an example to follow, especially with all her shortcomings in writing her projects! Her very spiritual journey included prayer, meditation, and attending chapel or a church service. My soul holds on to every word she wrote. Most saints don't disclose their inner thoughts like she does, whether they are true or not. Ever since I was a little girl, I knew things and could not understand how I knew those things. I felt I was a stranger in this world and the family I was born into. I loved people and understood their pains. As a small child, I had an innate knowing; an inner knowing of what others were going through in their soul. At one time in my life, I felt I may have needed more parental involvement to help channel my gifts, talents and abilities; especially my deep spiritual gifts that were a blessing to have, but I didn't understand. However, I realize that a parent can only teach their children what they know and are willing to explore themselves. Therefore, I had to forgive that illusion, resentment and false concept I held within my soul of my mother not being able to help me spiritually. The bags of hatred were too heavy and they burdened me down, so I let go. In order to fulfill my dreams as a child, at age 49, I really had to let those unwanted heavy bags go away.

While growing up, I always sensed another realm living around my soul. I was not conscious of the "Spirit world." I only heard about ghosts and s at Halloween. One day my friend, Rhonda, died (transitioned) in a train accident in the 9th grade. Rhonda's body was decimated into small pieces; she was always a big or chubby girl. I was skinny and I used to make fun of her even though she was a dear friend. Mourning and feeling guilty over her death I started asking her forgiveness even though she was dead. One night Rhonda appeared in my room perfect, whole and complete as a lighted Spirit. She told me she forgave me. I was frightened and glad, at the same time, to hear those words. This was one of the beginnings of my spiritual journey. While I was a young girl, other spiritual events happened to me, such as seeing angels the like. But, this one experience left an impact on my soul and taught me a valuable lesson. One thing was sure; it was not my imagination or a daydream, which is what my parents would have said if I had told them. I never spoke of this until I was an adult.

From that time on, my rational mind allowed me to express more mysticism in art, writing, imagination, modeling, creativity, dreams, paint, fashion and my language of inner knowing quietly. Why the quiet? Because I had no one who believed in me or talked to me about the things that were important to my soul. So I talked to non-physical beings. I knew they were present even when I was small. This was not my vivid imagination. As I lived in that dysfunctional home, I imagined myself writing, painting, modeling, having children later in life around my 30s and a career. This was happening around the age of twelve and on. This kept me focus and a little sane! After high school, I attended fashion and merchandising school, finishing all classes.

    Once I married, had six children. After ending that marriage, it was time to discover me! As written earlier, I wrote my second book as a result of dear friends pushing me to tell my story for others. I didn't know what to do. I didn't even do any research. I just shared the depths of my heart and my voice came out. I really didn't know how to voice my story; I just did it. Things were happening to me when I was in my forty–ninth year; it was my awakening. Many of the things that occurred shaped and formed the new character of who I am now! Remember, at this time I was not involved in a Center for Worship. The messages were being transmitted to my soul and mind telepathically. During that time, it felt so natural to me that I would think it was all me. My dear one, it wasn't me. It was my Guardian angels, both of them; man and woman. It was also my non-physical animal totems. I didn't know then that my non-physical teachers and guides were speaking to me. In this time of my life, I now know one for sure was always there connecting and guiding my soul for my well being. My soul teacher has always been my teacher, Saint Teresa of Avila. This incredibly gifted woman was born in Avila, Spain in 1515 and died in 1582. I didn't know her when I started my spiritual and personal transformation in my life in 2005, but she was aware of me. I know she was because my second book states a few of the same words that she used in *Interior Castle* (1946) and *My Book of Life* (2007). Saint Teresa was a Roman Catholic mystic, a Spanish nun, a writer, teacher and guide, a model of good and saint of all times. Years after her death, she became the first female to be named a doctor of the Catholic Church. In pure humility to her beloved, she served mankind in courage. Even though she is not in the physical body anymore, she still lights the pathway for those who want to serve their beloved and mankind if one can receive and be open to her timely messages. One message she is known for is her intimate prayer life with her beloved. Again, Mystic Charles Fillmore in *The Revealing Word* (1995) states intimate prayer life to be, "one who has an intimate first hand-acquaintance with God: a man (woman), of prayer." This relationship is not built upon a person going to another person to understand the things of God but to experience this devotion themselves. After reading this book, dear writer, are you one to develop an intimate time with the *Infinite Spirit*?

About the Saint from the 16th Century

After her rebellious acts when she was a teenager, she entered the convent at age eighteen with great hopes. Her mother died when she was twelve and the thoughts of children and marriage didn't cross her mind. Once she entered the convent it almost killed her. She did it for all the wrong reasons; to run away from life and the thoughts of marriage. Teresa was a beautiful woman; long shapely legs and the men of that time were in love with her youthful body and charm. Even way back then, she was a leader to whom all types of people would listen when she spoke. This included, women, men, King Phillip, ordinary people, bishops and more. She learned, and enjoyed, being in silence and solitude, as well as being with groups of people. Her laughter and humor was contagious. Saint Teresa could have married a fine man and had a wonderful family. However, this was not her life choice. Finally, she committed to her calling, released her confused mind from trying to fit into the world and accepted her dedication to please her beloved. She thought she could live a worldly life and be a nun at the same time. Nonetheless, this woman was very spiritual; however, she suffered many years and kept her faith.

She started to contemplate on the beauty of a soul in grace and thought how she could express the concept. Then, the Bishops approached her to write the treatise on prayer in which she specialized in daily. This is how her book *Interior Castle,* which is one of the Saint's better known literary works, was written. As she focused her thoughts toward how to start this book and how she may glorify her beloved, an answer was shown. God gave her heart's desires in due form and order. A subject was given unto her as she applied her mind in a prayer of thought. In a vision, she saw a crystal globe. In the globe, there was the shape of a castle with seven mansions inside it. The closer one got to the seventh mansion one could see it was where the *Infinite Spirit* resided. As a person got closer to the center of this particular mansion, the light was so strong and bright. There was even darkness around the outside of this mansion where dark infested creators lived. She likens this metaphor to our human life, how we are trying to get to the center of where the beloved resides, and yet we have a darkness surrounding us that we must detach from.

Her Writing Path

Back in the 16th century, women were not allowed to further their education. She would read from religious books on prayer and romance novels. These books became close acquaintances. Once her superiors heard about her strange spiritual life, the men in power thought her ways were from evil spirits. Even so, she was under inquisition for raptures she experienced, visions she saw and voices she heard. As she went through the unconventional spiritual life, the word spread throughout the countryside. The men in charge took her books on prayer and she felt alone; the books gave her much comfort. This Saint believed books served to help transform a person's life. The inquisition team challenged her spiritual ecstasy and they thought she was perhaps insane. What they didn't know was that she too questioned her own spiritual life whenever it happened to her. She sought answers from God to see if this was truly from Him. Once the team of men realized it was indeed a Divine Ecstasy, they asked her to write about her life and prayer. As a result, *The Book of My Life* (2007) was developed. Saint Teresa is the only nun on this Earth to teach both the nuns and the monks. At the age of forty, her mission as a writer was to teach; she had no concerns on keeping one just happy in her books. At this age, she started to wear the hat of a mystic. Teresa wrote the details of her experiences of her spiritual life. She did this writing so the men in charge would understand her spiritual life and know what she was about. Therefore, she passed the test, but not without discrimination and gossiping. This woman, who was a nun and mystic, is a fine example of how one should have courage when under the microscope of others who don't agree with your spiritual life. When the men in power took her books on prayer and romantic novels, which had become close to her soul, she heard the voice of God saying to her that He would replace her books with a living book. Also, God told her, "Don't be sad." Her passion was to read; this was her love. The only books the men would allow her to read were written in Latin and not Spanish, which was her language. This is when the Saint developed an appreciation of silence and the unknowing. If she had still had her books on prayer, she may not have been able to sit in silence. Her beloved became her living book.

"Don't be sad, I will give you a living book," God was told her. She didn't understand. Then her spiritual visions started. He took her into His arms and gave her assurance of His love. He taught her many things, and showed her many things, that she thought about over and over about what He taught. She had no need for books again. Her beloved became a Living Book to her. In her own words, she wrote in *The Book of My Life* (2007), "Blessed be such a book that indelibly imprints on our minds everything we need to understand and do!" (p. 197) Teresa, in all her undertaking, sought the Lord's help and to do his will. In the midst of her entire devotion, the nun faced illness daily for many years. While her spiritual manifestations were received daily from her beloved, she still lived in fear. Often Christ would come and sit by her in special gatherings and Chapel. She would also hear His voice speaking words of wisdom and assurance and also of what was to come. Finally, she gained trust in His words and carried out whatever He told her to do while in prayer. She still questioned where the voices were coming from, an evil Spirit or God. Some people in our day would think of her having a mental illness and low-self esteem. But once you read her mystical literary works, including *Interior Castle*, my favorite, you will know who she truly was.

I ask, "Can you develop your spiritual life and trust the process?" Put yourself in the Saints shoes. What would you have done when your spiritual life was being questioned? How would you have handled this? What would you do when the men in power came to you to write and you had no formal education? How would you exhibit courage in the middle of a personal storm? Would you write your secrets to your prayer life? How would feel if the *Infinite Spirit* appeared to you, sat by you, and welcomed you?

Write Your Thoughts Here

_____
_____
_____
_____
_____
_____
_____
_____
_____
_____

Her Mission

Saint Teresa reformed convents and created new monasteries as she traveled the back roads and countryside of Spain with her nuns. She wrote many books, faced many illnesses, developed contemplative prayer practices and delivered a universal message. Even though she was a devout Roman Catholic mystic, counseled kings, queens and rich people, and saw Christ, she wrote her last book around the age of sixty-five entitled *Interior Castle*. Don't forget she had a very different spiritual practice and maintained communion with her beloved. She left with us an example of good conversations from people, listening to inspired messages from the chapel, spinning, music, art, poetry and through books, according to Teresa, in sickness, prayer and meditation. Now that we are at the end, do you have your spiritual practice in place?

At one point when she wrote a book on prayer, the Superiors took it from her. It was called *Life*. In a conversation with a spiritual guide, P. Jeronimo Gracian, she was sharing how she discussed spiritual matters in the book, *Life*, in a better manner. He advised her to recall the information and write another book and to go to confessions with Dr. Velazquez and share this information; the book came to be called *Book of the Mansions*. She went to see Dr. Velazquez and he encouraged her to do the same. The Saint didn't want to write. She did anyway.

Whenever the Saint was ordered to write, she did, regardless of her confidence and humbleness. She asked Gracian, "Why do they want me to write things?" Have you ever, dear writer, asked this question when you were asked to write or do something similar? Then she told him,

> Let the learned men, who have studied, do the writing; I am a stupid creature and don't know what I am saying. There are more than enough books on prayer already. For the love of God, let me get on with my spinning and go to choir and do my religious duties like the other sisters. I am not meant for writing: I have neither the heath nor the wits for it.

Let's stop here and ponder her statement. This was a humble mystic nun who didn't think she was smart enough to write to others. Yet, she was a wonderful spiritual teacher who taught the nuns and the monks.

Nevertheless, she teaches us today. Those of us who have ears to hear, and eyes to read, her literary masterpieces. Her spiritual devotion was in communion with her beloved daily. Yet, she had a familiarity with doubts and fears. Her self-worth was so low that she thought of herself as stupid and she wasn't sure of what she was saying. She discounted herself and what she had to offer the world on prayer and a spiritual walk to draw closer to the beloved. If it was totally up to her, we wouldn't have any of her three books; not to mention the Christian mystical classic, *Way of Perfection* (1946).

Dear Writer

     You are reading this book because you desire to write a book under the influences of the *Infinite Spirit*. Your interest has been peaked and you know that you are called to bring forth a Divine message to the world. You have a profound message of insights from a personal experience, challenges and growth. You have a well plotted fiction story, healing and added health, science fiction story, Christian fiction, family memoirs, children's literature of non-fiction or fiction, Spiritual inspiration, etc. In spite all the information and experiences of reading of this book, some of you still have a few doubts and fears. My dears, a while back, I had doubts and fears as well, until I read Saint Teresa's books! Within the content of those pages, she is a real, down-to-Earth person with the self-imposed limitations she experienced. As I learned, she didn't want to write, neither did I at one point. I too thought I was not smart enough and didn't have anything to say to an audience. My thoughts were her thoughts "Let the learned men write... they are educated [more than I]". But I realized that the *Infinite Spirit* called me; not the learned men.

They had formal education and I did not. On the other hand, I knew that I was called to write regardless of my inner self-imposed limitations. She is a prime example of being obedient to the call to write and trusting in the *Infinite Spirit* for inner wisdom and knowledge to write. As she wrote, her soul became smaller and her beloved became larger; therefore, she gained spiritual consolations as she wrote. Never re-reading her works, she had a forgetful memory as she wrote. She couldn't remember what she wrote, plus she didn't proofread her works. Her writing style was always in a hurried pace. She felt a sense of imperfection. Often, when writing on her prayer life, she tried to hide the fact the she was the person she was writing about; the same remarkable woman who Christ sat by as she saw and talked with angels. He even spoke many comforting words to her soul and gave her inner assurances daily. He was her living book. However, this mystical nun only wrote what she knew best; her prayer life. She speaks here to you today: "I shall speak of nothing of which I have no experience, either in my own life or in observation of others, or which the Lord has not taught me in prayer."

    For those of you who are ready to enter into dedication with the *Infinite Spirit*, it's your season now! You have the roadmap inside this book. I would invite you to reread the text for a spiritual understanding and how to evoke the presence of the Divine and unseen beings into your literary works. You are ready for this knowledge and the tools are present. Set the time aside to get familiar with your non-physical writing assistants. You are that chosen vessel; a channel of light for the works to come through you to change the world. When you get lost or distracted, just start over in a meditation and prayer inviting your non-physical assistants to source you with knowledge from on high. Be sure, when awakened, to get up and be ready to write. Then do it; don't procrastinate. When the non-physical assistants are nudging you, use the free energy and guidance for your book projects. Enter into the silence and meditation to make contact with the *Infinite Spirit*. You are a channel, a writing vessel.

"Let nothing disturb you, nothing frighten you. All things are passing. God never changes. Patient endurance will attain to all things; Who God possesses, in nothing is wanting; Alone God suffices."
–Saint Teresa

Afterthought

Since reading and editing this book, I fully understand everything does happen for a reason. As a freelance graphic designer and editor, it was my duty to read every single word, phrase and sentence to verify that it makes complete sense to you, the reader. I have to digest every word and sentence to understand the author's Spirit and thoughts and how it communicates to you. Therefore, I not only edited the book, I read it thoroughly as well. I ingested each thought and each experience, then I applied myself, as if I was the one purchasing this book. It was important that I understood and applied the concepts and experiences within my Spirit so that I understood how to make sure the author's communication to you made sense.

    As far as how much the book has impacted me, it has helped me to understand how powerful thoughts and words can be to others and to me. It has solidified how powerful the atom of thought manifested by Multi-verse/God can be, which can have powerful actions. Before, I was troubled with many issues of my past and I had allowed them to take precedence in my present life; however, with mentioning the journal writing in the book, taking responsibility for your actions, and understanding the purposes it had for learning, this was my confirmation that I am on the right track with beginning my journal writing again. It also gave me more confidence in my editing skills. I played the victim role of what everyone was doing to ME, but not realizing that I am creating the problem by allowing it to occur with my thoughts. I figured out, through my journal writing, that words can be truthful and hurtful; yet, rewarding and healing at the same time when seen on paper. I was able to confront my fears, look at my mistakes, analyze them and then put them aside as a lesson learned and move forward. It has helped me realize how much potential I have and that my words and skills can help others change lives.

Therefore, my final thought is to digest this book within your Spirit and understand what purpose it has for you. You purchased this book for a reason. Seek the answers, and then write about it so that others can grow from you. This is the way of spiritual truth.
--Lauren Johnson, Freelance graphic designer/editor

My husband and I recently took Carol's writing workshop where we were so inspired by not only what Carol knows about writing books, but her method of tapping into her Higher Power to do so. Carol's enthusiasm is infectious. Her knowledge and tips are invaluable. As a result, we just published our first book called "Comfort from Heaven"! Thank you Carol!
-Annie and Ralph Tagg, Angel Cottage

I attended Carol's "Writing with the Infinite Spirit" workshop on Sunday, 25 Mar 2012, at the Unity Church in Nashville, TN. Driving there, I did not know what to expect because I was following up on an invite as published in the Tennessee Tribune newspaper. I even wondered it this was some sort of spiritual retreat. Once there, the light was bright, I felt very welcomed, and the atmosphere was inspiring to all.

Carol possesses a unique energy that motivates others in immeasurable ways. This workshop was educational, "audience-involving" and it allowed me to reach within and extract the buried beauty. As she pointed out, each of us wear a mask that limits our prosperity. She went further by passing the mask around and having each person admit the particulars of the mask worn that stunts our growth. The knowledge poured during Carol's workshop overfilled my cup and my advice for future attendees: be prepared to accept it all.

Filled with "Infinite" vigor as I drove home, I thought about the direction of my writings, subject for additional work, marketing techniques and information sharing. I thought about ways to aid others in "releasing their mask" of limitations. Throughout this week, I have been restless, absorbing refreshed ideas and settling into a renewed me. I am still very pumped and hyped, to say the least.

- Joe Shakeenab, Philosophical Poet, Author of two books to be released this summer: *Somalia, Moments of Visions and Voices* and *A Widow's Son, Philosophical Enlightenment*

About the Author

Carol S. Batey, Ph.D.
Doctor of Metaphysics, Lifestyle Coach
Motivational Speaker

Published Works:
Parents Are Lifesavers!
In Due Season: Destiny's Calling Your Soul
Poise for the Runway of Your Life
What's Cooking in Your Soul?
Why Aren't You Writing?
Developing a Mystic Consciousness
Phone: 615-485-4548
Email: Carol37076@aol.com
Website: www.artlifestylecoach.com

Carol Batey, Ph.D., author, Doctor of Metaphysics and lifestyle coach, is the mother of six children. She is the author of numerous magazine and newspaper articles. Her book *Parents Are Lifesavers* supports those educators and parent-leaders looking to increase parent involvement! In December 2010, she was featured as an expert in *Ebony* on how to help children set goals for the new year.

Her second book, *In Due Season: Destiny's Calling Your Soul*, recaps the events that occurred in the past two and a half years as she approached her 50th birthday. The unwrapping of her soul was unveiled, changing her into the person she is today. Now, she is willing to share this inspirational message of reinventing herself with her readers and seekers of personal transformation. Carol faced fibromyalgia and overcomes it as she shares her journey within this book.

In *Poise for the Runway of Your Life* she shares her passions, personal revelations, insights, victories and how she regained her balance and poise through her life's changes and lessons. Upon the demise of her twenty-one year marriage and her sole career as a homemaker, she made the conscious choice to embrace and purse the passions of her heart to model, teach metaphysics and write.

Carol's latest project, released in September of 2010, is entitled *What's Cooking in your Soul?* The readers are asked this question because most people don't take the time to find out. Carol takes her readers on a journey of introspection that allows each person to come out with their own secret ingredient in their spiritual and personal transformation. This book also features Carol's one of a kind Vibration Cooking and recipes! Total healing can be achieved through all of her works.

Carol's signature workshops are *Your Destiny Awaits You!*, *Unlocking Your Potential to Write Books* and *Why Aren't You Writing?* Carol recently received her doctoral degree in Mystical Research. Her latest offering is *Developing a Mystic Consciousness* for those seeking a higher spiritual awakening.

Carol's fifth book, *Writing with the Infinite Spirit*, helps open up one's potential to write books.

Carol's Mission

"Destiny is not a matter of chance it is a matter of choice, it is not a thing to be waited for; it is a thing to be achieved."
- William Jennings Bryant (1860-1925)

Carol's personal mission: When she is conducting metaphysical coaching, she uses lessons from the life skills she learned and developed to empower women, men and children to use their potential on their life's journey. After putting herself in her students' and readers' traveling shoes, covering the miles upon miles they will need to reach their ultimate inner goal or personal transformation, she helps them map their paths. Many have asked how to make time to accomplish their purpose and where the money will come from. To uncover your personal transformation, you first start with a desire to create. Next, a spiritual practice of meditating, fasting and prayer, journaling, being still and listening and physical exercising and proper nutrients will help you start your transformation.

Are you ready to travel the runway of your life? By using the power within and metaphysics, you can have a spiritual and personal transformation!

Examine your ego, as I did, to discover your desires and reasons for wanting to change and make a resolution to do the hard work necessary to get physically, spiritually, emotionally and mentally fit. My goal was to create a new Carol. What is your goal? Do you need or want newness within?

The labor and the miles I traveled weren't as hard once I surrendered and gave into the Universal Spirit's laws. The Law of Attraction and Allowing! The principles in my books are what I use to coach classes. They are tried, tested and proven true if your heart and soul are open and your Spirit and mind are willing. Are you willing?

With the Master Creator's divine help we can awaken our minds, bodies and souls to remember our divine purpose here on Earth at this time. Seeking the Divine's help by asking for assistance from the *Infinite Spirit* is where we start first, since we are co-creators in our destiny. Take this time to remember your soul's divine purpose.

All of my books are catalysts for change if you are open to finding the buried treasures within your soul, Spirit and mind. The principles mentioned will nourish and direct your path and soul. Then, the power of God will start to transform your life. The Spirit's guidance will be felt within your life and soul, surrounding you by directing your path daily. Learn to let go, surrender to the Universal God and the Laws of the Earth; "The Law of Attraction and Allowing." You will inherit joy, peace, wisdom, abundant living and a new purpose in life. You will create unity with your God. This is my mission for all who are ready and willing to receive.

Acknowledgements

In heartfelt thanks, I would also like to give hats off to www.WhereAngelsTakeFlight.com publisher Debra Lynn Katz!

Made in the USA
Columbia, SC
20 March 2025